SPINNING BENEATH MY FEET

AN IRISHMAN TREKS TO THE NORTH POLE

Resolute Devon Island

70°N

ALAN HUMPHRIES & DAVID WECKER

WITH A BRIEF HISTORY OF IRISH POLAR EXPLORATION

Published by Alan Humphries and David Wecker
© Alan Humphries and David Wecker 2010

ISBN 978-0-9566503-0-6
First Edition
First impression

Designed by April Sky Design, Newtownards
www.aprilsky.co.uk

Spinning Beneath My Feet

Best Wishes

ALAN HUMPHRIES & DAVID WECKER

CONTENTS

Polar Exploration is a most isolated way of ha... way of ... yet been...

"Polar Exploration is at once the
cleanest and most isolated way
of having a bad time that has
yet been devised."

… Apsley Cherry-Garrard

Chapter 1

INTRODUCTION

The drone of the Twin Otter engines was receding in the distance as I gazed at the frozen landscape surrounding me. For the first time, I felt the biting cold, inescapable and merciless, and a heavy sense of isolation. The world as I knew it was far, far away. The only way to get back to it was to go forward, north to the top of the world. Having just stepped out of the relative warm comfort of the aeroplane and into the savage Arctic cold, I swallowed hard. One thought echoed in my mind:

"We'd better get this over as quickly as possible."

When you mention you've been to the North Pole, it begs the question: Why?"

All I can say is, if you have to ask the question, you wouldn't understand the answer.

One other question comes to mind as well:

Which pole?

In point of fact, there are five poles, each a reflection of a phenomenon or condition of the planet that someone wanted to measure. They are:

The frozen Landscape of the North Pole is not the place for the faint-hearted

- **The North Pole** of inaccessibility, defined as the farthest point in the Arctic from the nearest coast in any direction. At the time of this writing, that distance was 684 miles.
- **The magnetic North Pole**, where the compass points. This point is always shifting from one point to another in the Canadian Arctic.
- **The celestial North Pole,** an astronomical extension of an imaginary line that constitutes the axis of the earth – one that in extension narrowly misses the North Star.
- **The geomagnetic North Pole** is the epicentre of the earth's magnetic field, located over northwest Greenland.
- **The geographical North Pole,** the big daddy of all the poles. It is my quest for this pole that this book is about. This is the pole that, for centuries, eluded even the hardiest, most resourceful explorers. It's defined simply as 90 degrees north.

From this pole, all points are south. It is, indeed, the top of the world, a place completely empty of anything resembling civilization or, for that matter, our planet as we understand it. It is a place that is beyond and, in a way, above all civilization.

Ninety North is a mathematical abstract, a set of scientific coordinates that direct the imagination to a phantom-like place on the planet that exists somewhere in the 5,000,000-square-mile expanse of the constantly shifting Arctic Sea. There, the landscape never stops moving, one sheet shoving with immeasurable force against another in either a never-ending upheaval or a pulling apart. The ice may seem solid, but the sea beneath it is in perpetual motion.

Arctic explorer Paul Schurke (pronounced SURE-key) had mushed his way to the Pole four times when I accompanied him on his fifth trip. He poetically compares finding this North Pole to trying to stand on the shadow of a bird hovering overhead.

"Standing at the top of the world," he said, "is like walking across the face of God. Wispy cirrus clouds the rest of the world sees at 50,000 feet seem almost within reach.

"It's as if the firmaments are pressed down upon you."

To achieve the North Pole on foot, hauling your supplies on dogsled, you have to overcome an inordinate variety of obstacles in a terrain that is rarely anything other than hostile. What follows are descriptions of some of the hazards of

Twin Otter landing at the Resolute Bay

Mawson; Schurkes most
experienced dog

Makwa; my favourite dog in the team

high Arctic travel.

The ice is always moving. When it pulls apart, into a "lead," it can do so beneath your feet and swallow you up in water that, against the vivid white of everything else under the sky, is a shimmering black; the colour of onyx.

When a lead opens perpendicularly to your forward path, you have a choice. You can find a way to bridge it or walk to either to the left or the right until you find where it has closed again. But that can be like walking to the end of a rainbow, because leads can fizzle out after a few hundred feet or stretch on for hundreds of miles.

As immense sheets of ice weighing hundreds of millions of tons push together from the shifting seas beneath, pressure ridges can heave up like craggy mountains 30 and more feet into the air. Here again, if a pressure ridge is in your path, you can go over it or try to find a way around it. The most efficient approach is to take it head-on, but it requires shouldering a 1,200-pound dog sled up and over, risking broken bones in the process for both dogs and mushers.

Then there's the temperature. At the Pole, the mercury routinely drops to 70 below zero – roughly three times as cold as it gets in your kitchen freezer. It's a cold so cold, it burns; so cold that, should you fall into an open lead, the Arctic Sea actually feels warm. That's because the water isn't freezing. It's right around 32 degrees Fahrenheit or zero degrees Celsius. So if you do fall in, it's by far warmer than you've been probably for days or weeks.

It's when you climb out of the water that the trouble begins.

Your breath leaves you. The feeling is as if your wind has in an instant been sucked out of you. Your body wants to curl up from a loss of muscle control and the onslaught of violent, uncontrollable shivering. If you just stand there, exposed parts will freeze in about four minutes. You lose consciousness in about seven. After that, you have maybe 12 minutes before you freeze to death.

With the biting temperatures come whiteouts, intense blizzard conditions where the snow is so thick and fast, you can't see more than your arm's length in front of you. Facing into winds that gust up to 40 miles an hour, I felt the sensation in the whiteouts I experienced of trudging uphill. Even when the wind isn't blowing, one faces the threat of snow-blindness brought on by the sun's rays reflected against a world of mirrors the size of grains of sand.

Then there's a peril that can think, react and kill. The polar bear is the largest of all land predators. An adult male on his hind legs can easily stand 11 feet tall. I've heard whisperings from Cree and Inuit hunters of polar bears that spend their entire lives in the sea – feeding, mating, raising their young, always swimming, never climbing up onto the ice or, farther south, dry land. Such bears are said to attain heights of 15 feet, with six-inch claws capable of ripping the hide of a walrus.

All these hazards conspire to make even the simplest task a hundred times more difficult. Consider the simple act of going to the bathroom. You learn not to dally. Forget about toilet paper. We had no space in our packs for such frivolous items. Instead, we used snowballs. It's invigorating, but you get used to it. Besides, there's no time for the sort of contemplation associated with, say, reading the newspaper.

It was the April of 1999. I was part of a crew of 10 adventurers, all Arctic rookies that Schurke had agreed to lead to 90 North. We were an unlikely assortment of self-made types, each ticking off items on his or her life list, each completely unprepared for the unimaginable nature of the rigours we were about to face.

Our group included a brother-and-sister team of Florida orthodontists, an L.A. assistant prosecutor, a retired civil engineer from Minnesota, a Florida real estate developer, the owner of an auto repair shop in Michigan, the CEO of a major retail food chain, a Cincinnati-based inventor of new product concepts

Sled dogs are the 'work horses' of the Arctic

for some of the world's most powerful conglomerates and me, Alan Humphries, an entrepreneur who had done moderately well with a string of gaming outlets in Northern Ireland.

Schurke's itinerary called for us to reach the North Pole in three weeks. He chose April as the time to embark on our expedition. It was a case of good news, bad news.

The good news is that the weather tends to be less severe in the Arctic spring, with daylight around the clock. The bad news is that the ice is at its most active, pulling apart, creating leads capable of abruptly halting progress. It was a handful of good and a handful of bad.

We had no guarantees we would arrive at our goal, given all that could go wrong, the uncertainties of the weather and the fact that, now that we'd been dropped off on the ice, we were beginning to realise how tiny we were against the seemingly infinite backdrop of this frozen wilderness.

Working in our favour were the 18 Canadian Inuit sled dogs that would pull tirelessly to help us get there. To their harnesses, we attached two sleds loaded with supplies necessary to see us through the days ahead. Out of respect for them, I am including their names here.

Pulling my sled were Palasi, Rock, Carhart, Giggles, Ellesmere, Baffin, Makwa and my lead dog, Narpa. One point of interest was that Ellesmere and Baffin were brothers from the same litter and would run only when harnessed side by side.

The dogs pulling the other sled were Atti, Dusty, Otis, Beaufort, Sydney, Mawson, Lumi and in the lead, Slava.

Five years earlier, on a winter survival trek in Northern Minnesota, my sled dogs had included Mawson, as well as Ellesmere and Bafffin. Mawson had been a junior dog then, but by this time he was one of the top dogs in the pecking order.

These extraordinary animals function at their peak under the most horrendous conditions. While we had the relative luxury of our tents and sleeping bags, our dogs slept in the howling wind and snow and were ready to pull hard again with each new day. In fact, the only whining I heard during the entire expedition was from various two-legged members of our entourage.

The Inuit sled dog breed is considered the Sherman Tank of the mushing world. The dogs developed with the Arctic cultures that employed them as draft animals.

Evidence suggests that the nomadic Chukchi tribe of Siberia relied on dogs to pull sledges as early as 50 BC. The Chukchi still live in a part of the world where the severe cold makes survival a constant struggle. These people live through a combination of herding reindeer and hunting for bear, seal, walrus and fish.

The Chukchi were forced by circumstances to invent a means of travel that would give them ready access to various food sources, one superior to those of competing Arctic tribes. The sled dog was their answer. The animal is bred to cover long distances quickly, with a minimal amount of food – and to perform with an unquenchable desire to pull.

Over time, most of the other northern Asiatic tribes – among them, the Samoyeds, Tungus, Koryaks, Gilyaks and Kamchadals – harnessed dogs to sledges. This enabled them to extend their hunting range. The dogs also helped track their quarry, assisted in the attack, then hauled the kill home.

Sled dogs also furthered trade, making it possible for these Ice Age tribes to migrate back and forth across the frozen Bering Strait to North America, into what would become known as Alaska and Canada. Actual records of trade routes involving sled dogs in the sub-Arctic were taken by a 14th century Arab merchant trading a few hundred miles from the present site of Moscow.

Canadian Inuit dogs were clearly the mainstay of Arctic transport for a few thousand years. But when the snowmobiling frenzy swept the Arctic in the late '60s, the dogs fell into disuse, and the breed all but disappeared.

Fresh polar bear tracks put the dogs on alert

In recent years, however, these dogs are making a comeback in Greenland and the eastern Arctic as villagers have taken a renewed interest in this central element of their cultural heritage.

These dogs absolutely live to pull. Their pulling instinct is so strong that they need little training. Young dogs are first harnessed at about eight months of age. Each one is teamed alongside a seasoned veteran for training. But within minutes, they dig their feet in and their line goes taut as their intense pulling instinct clicks on like a light switch.

Because of their strength and ability to thrive in extreme conditions, Canadian Inuit dogs were selected to power the first expeditions to reach the North Pole, purportedly with Robert Peary in 1909, and to the South Pole, with Roald Amundsen in 1911. They have been employed on virtually all non-mechanised polar expeditions since.

Canadian Inuit Dogs are one of four main working breeds of the far north, which also includes the Siberian husky, the Malamute and the Samoyed.

The Siberian husky and their mixed breed cousins, commonly called Alaskan huskies, are the fastest and so is the breed of choice for racers, though they range from only 40 to 60 pounds in weight.

The Samoyed people of the Russian Arctic developed the breed named after them. But during the last century, European and American dog lovers were more attracted by the breed's beautiful white coat, and today Samoyeds are more commonly found on the pet show circuit than in harness.

Malamutes are the largest of the pulling dogs, typically weighing more than 100 pounds. They were developed by the Malamute people of western Alaska, a culture that no longer exists, and became famous for pulling the '49ers and their supplies over the Dawson Trail during the Alaskan Gold Rush, into the Yukon of Robert

Service's writings. They remain popular today as family pets and pulling dogs. But because their size makes them unwieldy for novice mushers to handle, they're rarely used for recreational dogsled programs.

The Canadian Inuit dog falls between the Malamute and Husky in size, with an average weight of about 80 pounds. They have the beef and build for back country travel but can still be comfortably handled by most beginners. Most are extremely personable and would never knowingly snap at a person, not in my experience anyway.

Like their cousins the Arctic wolves, they have extremely strong pack instincts. The pack hierarchy is always changing. Many of them will not run together without sparring over dominance. Reading these changes in the pack hierarchy and pairing the dogs up appropriately is part of the challenge and mystery of working with these amazing animals.

Working with a team of eight dogs is like working with a team of eight people from different planets. Each has his or her needs, abilities and personalities. They'll work together and get the job done, but maximising their performance requires strong leadership. That's what mushing is all about. You basically become the coach of a team of Olympic-calibre athletes.

And they truly are athletes. An Inuit dog will pull at least twice its weight in payload at a pace of six to eight miles an hour for hours at a time. Their thick double coats and tough demeanour enable them to thrive in extreme conditions. In fact, the colder it is, the harder they pull. They're accustomed to eating snow for moisture and, when night comes, they curl into a ball, wrap their tails over their noses, settle into the snow and sleep soundly. Come daybreak, they all pop up with the slightest hint around camp that sleds are being loaded, anxiously pawing the air as if seeking to be the first to be harnessed.

Over the coming weeks, we would come to depend on the dogs for more than just their pulling ability. The bond between man and these specialised animals dates back to the beginning of recorded history.

These dogs also became protectors and companions, again aiding in the survival of humans. They warned of approaching polar bears and, more importantly, developed a remarkable capability to find a safe way in the path ahead. There is documented proof that sled dogs have detected crevasses in the ice field while finding crossings with solid bases, where their human masters could not.

It may be that the greatest value these animals provide, especially to the lone hunter, is that they bond so completely with people, offering a source of comfort, morale and well being.

It was that way for David Oingoot, a 59-year-old Inuit who lives off the land around Resolute, a tiny village that has become the jumping-off point for polar expeditions from the Western hemisphere and served as the base camp for Cincinnati newspaper columnist David Wecker, our base camp manager and link back to civilization.

David Oingoot hunts seals and musk ox to feed his family. Occasionally, he leads wealthy hunters from other parts of the world on polar bear hunts. On the day we met, he was mourning the loss of two of his sled dogs.

He said he never goes looking for polar bears without at least 10 dogs. On this occasion, he'd just returned from such a hunt after five days on the sea ice.

"Dogs are good for a few reasons," David said, speaking in the native Inuktitut language of the Inuit, with his 31-year-old son Adam translating.

"They make different sounds, depending. If they hear a bear, it's yip, then a few seconds, then another yip. If they smell a bear, they growl, and they turn and follow that bear. If they see a bear, it's a growl, then a deep steady barking."

When an Inuit hunter comes upon a bear, he turns his dogs loose. The bear David brought back from this hunt was more than 11 feet tall, with a dark muzzle, which the Inuit regard as a sign of an especially dangerous bear.

"The dogs, they go through a lot of punishment," David said.

"What we can fix, we fix. But this bear had a black muzzle. He snapped the spines of two of my dogs. It's hard to shoot your dog. Very hard."

For me, the dogs were a source of inspiration. As we stood there on the ice, they seemed as eager as any of us to get to the Pole. I didn't want to do anything to slow them down.

Arctic fire beautiful fla...
its orange glow its flick...
burns keeping darkness ...
ows until break of day...
smoldering timber. Warm...
Arctic winter.

Arctic fire,
beautiful flame comfort in the night,
its orange glow,
its flickering light .
The heart that burns keeping darkness at bay
Lighting the shadows until break of day
The crackling tinder
The smoldering timber
Warming the bones from this Arctic winter.

… Alan Humphries at age 14

Chapter 2

CHASING A DREAM

As early as I can remember, winter was my season; nothing quite excited me as much as the first snowfall of each new winter. It was a feeling, I imagine, similar to the feeling some get on a bright summer morning or a crisp autumn afternoon. It was almost an intoxicating feeling, a joyful sense of exhilaration. For some reason, snow got me going. It got me excited. I felt at home in its whiteness and cold.

One of my earliest and most distinct memories was of a dark winter morning when I was 8 years old, riding with my dad in his delivery truck to Londonderry. The snow was falling thick and heavy, and the headlights of the truck were lighting up each flake as it fell. I remember losing myself in the flurry that was happening on the other side of the windshield, almost being hypnotized by it.

I'd heard the stories of such polar explorers as Robert Falcon Scott, whose ill-fated expedition to the South Pole cost the lives of his team of five men. But somehow gazing into the snow falling in our headlights at that moment made me understand that explorer mindset in a way I never had before. It made me want to explore the poles myself.

One of my most memorable childhood toys was an Action Man Explorer set. Action Man, if you don't know, was sort of a soldier action figure for boys. My particular Action Man was outfitted with a polar parka with fur-trimmed hood, a team of three plastic husky sled dogs and a plastic sled.

I spent hours and hours creating snowy scenarios for Action Man from polystyrene foam. My older brother, Brian, was quite inventive in terms of helping me shape landscapes. It remains a hobby for him to this day, recreating battle scenarios in miniature, from the American Civil War in particular, but also from the

Resolute Bay

Napoleonic Wars, World War II and Vietnam. He has sculpted tabletop battlefields complete with rivers, mountains, bridges and villages using such materials as sand, glue and foam rubber.

I was drawn to the dogs – one was grey and white, the second red and white and the third black and white. Years later, the first Siberian husky sled dogs I would own would have those same markings.

I came by my fascination with exploration honestly, having inherited it from my maternal grandfather, William Watson. A World War I veteran, he was never an explorer himself, but he loved reading about the great expeditions and the men who made them happen – and he found a ready audience in his daughter's third son. He introduced me to the stories of Jack London and delighted in reciting the poetry of Robert Service, especially after he'd had a couple of jars.

As a child, I would stay with my grandparents during the day while my mother worked at the linen mill. Some of my most vivid memories are of him in his armchair by an open fireplace, me sitting cross-legged on the floor and listening attentively as he recited "The Shooting of Dan McGrew."

Even at my tender age, it was clear to me McGrew had it coming. At the same time, I was swept away with a longing to see and experience that faraway frozen wilderness of the north for myself. Service's verses set my boyhood antenna to twitching. Verses such as the one below ignited my imagination.

> *Were you ever out in the Great Alone,*
> *when the moon was awful clear*
> *And the icy mountains hemmed you in*
> *with a silence you most could hear;*
> *With only the howl of a timber wolf,*
> *and you camped there in the cold,*
> *A half-dead thing in a stark, dead world,*
> *clean mad for the muck called gold;*
> *While high overhead, green, yellow and red,*
> *the North Lights swept in bars?*
> *Then you've a hunch what the music meant*
> *… hunger and night and the stars.*

In London's stories, too, there was always a dog – that great icon of the north, the sled dog. I loved my Action Man explorer and trio of plastic sled dogs, but more than anything, I wanted a dog of my own. It would be some time before my parents acquiesced to this wish. However, for a brief time, I did have a pet – a tom turkey. I saw him only once, 10 days before Christmas. He was living in the garage where my dad worked.

I remember being practically beside myself at finally having a little pet of my own. I petted him, I hugged him and I asked if I might take him for a wee walk. I was disappointed when my father put me off. "Not now," he said. "Next time, maybe."

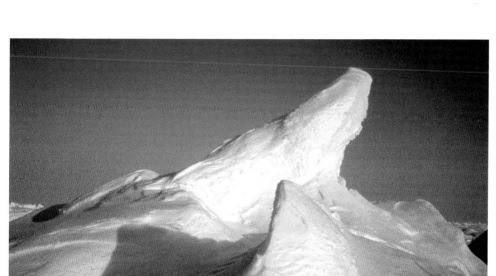

A wind cut ice sculpture

I never saw my beloved tom turkey again – not in his feathered state, at least. The episode only intensified my longing to have a dog of my own.

In the summer of 1989, I bought two fine Siberian huskies. Nouska had a black-and-white mask, a sweet disposition and a strong will. Skiba was one of her litter sisters – with a mask of red and white and a more passive temperament than her sister. They died at the ripe old ages of 18 and 15, respectively.

They were 10-week-old pups when I got them. I purchased them from a breeder in the south of England. As far as I knew, they were the first Siberian huskies in Northern Ireland.

By the time they were 10 months old, I was running them in harness pulling a mountain bicycle, with a line attached to the bike's front fork. They pulled side by side, but Nouska always insisted on being in front by at least a nose.

I didn't have to train them – they pulled from instinct and at a good clip through Hillsborough Forest Park near my Northern Ireland home. I'd help out a bit with pedalling up hills, but it was easy riding for me the rest of the time. They were strong pullers, both of them.

In the autumn of '93, I learned about Paul Schurke through a small advertisement he placed in a dogsled enthusiast magazine for his Wintergreen Lodge in Ely, Minn. The ad described a wintertime survival course Schurke was offering. Participants would take two weeks to cross the Boundary Waters of the northern Minnesota wilderness with dogsleds. I signed up immediately, without knowing anything about who this Schurke fellow was.

On the trip from Belfast to Ely, I stopped in Duluth, Minn., and happened into a bookshop, where I discovered a couple books Schurke had written – including his

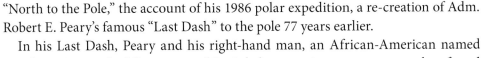

"North to the Pole," the account of his 1986 polar expedition, a re-creation of Adm. Robert E. Peary's famous "Last Dash" to the pole 77 years earlier.

In his Last Dash, Peary and his right-hand man, an African-American named Matthew Henson, had four personal Inuit helpers, natives more commonly referred to by what they themselves regard as the pejorative term, Eskimo.

Peary, Henson and the rest of their party followed behind a team of 18 seasoned explorers with 100 of their own dogs, all blazing a trail in stages to the pole. Peary, Henson and their four helpers were able to save their energy while the rest of the team did most of the grunt work, hacking out a trail through the ice rubble and creating passes over pressure ridges that stood 30 feet high and higher.

The expedition – Peary's third with Henson since 1900 – began on Ellesmere Island at the edge of the Arctic Ocean in the spring of 1909, about 420 nautical miles (or 483 miles) from the pole, building igloos each day. By travelling at the rear of the pack, Peary was able to travel lightly, limiting his sled weight to 400 pounds for his final dash of about 150 miles as the crow flies. Of course, the frozen Arctic conditions seldom allow for linear travel – requiring forward progress to be far more often than not a matter of zigzagging painfully this way and that, covering as much as six miles of ice to make a single mile of actual progress.

Word that Peary had arrived at the North Pole didn't reach America until the following September, when the New York Times published a story with the headline, "Peary Discovers the North Pole after Eight Trials in 23 Years."

For the next seven decades, it was generally accepted that Peary had indeed discovered the pole – until 1988, when the National Geographic Society, one of the chief sponsors of his expeditions, had his records re-examined and decided that the explorer's evidence didn't prove his claim and further indicated he knew he hadn't made it.

The controversy continues, but none of it fazed me. I was excited at the prospect of spending the next 14 days with a genuine polar explorer.

It was early in March 1994. Suddenly, there I was, sleeping in the snow in temperatures that dipped as low as 25 below, loving every bit of it. The first morning, I woke up with eight inches of snow on my sleeping bag. I quickly crawled out and took a photo of the bag, snow and all.

Around the campfire each night, a woman who reminded me of Klinger from "M*A*S*H" would recite one of Robert Service's poems. She seemed to know all of them by heart. It was moments like those that reinforced my feeling this was where I belonged, sitting next to a fire outdoors in the heart of winter.

Each night, we were serenaded by a pack of wolves. We howled at them, and they howled back. Toward the end of the trip, as I was crossing a frozen lake, standing at the edge of the lake, straight ahead, was a large black wolf. We made eye contact and, a moment later, he casually trotted off into the woods. I still have the photograph I took of the wolf's paw print next to my hand. My hand fit easily into hollow its paw left in the snow.

I learned how to keep warm in sub-zero conditions, how to decipher signs of danger, how to navigate by the stars. By the end of the course, I felt ready to take the next step, whatever it would take to move me closer to the ultimate challenge of travelling to the North Pole on foot, hauling my supplies with a dogsled. I told Schurke to let me know if he ever decided to plan another trip to 90 North. He gave me his word.

The following winter, in February 1995, I hired a dog team in the northern Canadian town of Moosenee, a Cree Indian village at the bottom end of Hudson Bay. My guide, Carmen Tozer, took us on a 600-mile excursion across the frozen James Bay.

For two weeks on the trail, our diet consisted of moose – moose jerky, moose stew, moose curry and moose steaks. While I was busy gathering wood and making camp at the end of each day, Carmen would head off with his compound bow and return an hour or so later with something to put on the fire, usually a rabbit or a ptarmigan. But mostly, we ate moose. If there had been such a thing as moose muffins, we would have had them, too. It was enough moose for me – but my appetite for the Great White North continued to grow.

On my return to Northern Ireland, I became active in dogsled racing. At a time trial in Finland, I qualified for the World Championship Sprint Dogsled Race, an event held once every four years, drawing teams from every cold corner of the world, from Patagonia to Alaska.

Being from Ireland, I was sort of an equivalent to the Jamaican bobsledding team – a fish out of my natural water. My goal was not to finish last, and I achieved it. I was third from last. In my defence, I was forced by United Kingdom quarantine restrictions from using my own team and so had to hire a team of Finnish dogs. They were quick, but our lack of experience together had us at a disadvantage. Still, I was pleased to have finished ahead of the teams from Germany and the Czech Republic.

I stayed in touch with Schurke. In the autumn of 1997, he called to say he was planning an excursion to the Pole. It would be another re-creation of Peary's "Last Dash," this time leading a bunch of mostly high Arctic rookies.

Schurke knew my experience with the dogs would come in handy, which in turn would be helpful to the neophytes. His plan was to travel by foot and cross-country ski, using his Inuit sled dogs to haul the necessary provisions.

My response was almost instant: "OK, let's go." I didn't have to think about it.

Realising the trip required extensive training, I set about to getting myself in shape mentally and physically for the rigours of high Arctic. I purchased a set of ridiculous roller-skis – skis roughly a third of the length of normal cross-country skis, with rollerblade rollers at either end – and embarked on a free weights training program with my older brother, Brian.

We trained five days a week for the better part of a year, with occasional breaks for holidays and the like. For three of those days, we did a complete regimen. The other two days were more of what I think of as an executive workout, primarily involving extended stretches in the Jacuzzi.

Our first
pressure ridge

In the three months leading up to our departure, I stepped it up some, to the point where I was doing 10 miles a day on the roller-skis. I also took half a dozen winter camping trips with my dogs in the Mourne Mountains, Ireland's highest mountain range.

During this time, I saw an opportunity to use the upcoming expedition to raise money for a good charity. My Aunt Betty Humphries was struggling with cancer at the time, so I settled on Action Cancer. Enlisting support from primary schools throughout Northern Ireland, we were able to raise more than £5,000, which went directly to the cancer fund.

Action Cancer posted a press release about my efforts. Soon I was receiving requests from newspapers, TV and radio stations for interviews. My favourite was a piece with the local BBC channel that featured one of my Siberian huskies. In general, I was pleasantly surprised and grateful for the coverage; the media made me look good. You can see for yourself – clips of some of the newspaper articles, both before and after the expedition, are reproduced in the back of this volume.

In an effort to draw attention to and perhaps raise funds for Action Cancer, I set about to looking for ways to put my polar expedition together with a corporate sponsor. For Bushmills Whisky, I dreamed up a "Bush on Ice" campaign. And Guinness had a new product at the time called Guinness Extra Cold that I thought would be a perfect fit.

I contacted the advertising firms for both products and made my pitches, to no avail. If I were doing it again, I'd go straight to the corporate marketing departments. In any case, my ideas must have had some substance because, a couple years later,

Guinness launched a successful advertising campaign called "Believe" based on the exploits of the Irish polar explorer, Tom Crean.

Schurke summoned the members of the expedition to his lodge in northern Minnesota for a 10-day team training session in December 1998, about five months prior to our scheduled departure. It was my first opportunity to meet the other members of what would come to be called the Aspirations Expedition. They were:

- **Bill Martin,** 49, an orthodontist from Gainesville, Fla., who met me at the airport outside Ely. Martin was a wilderness medicine expert and mountaineer, a decent fellow always up for a laugh.
  Martin had led climbing expeditions in North and South America, Russia, Irian Jaya and the Himalayas. In 1986, he was part of the second climbing expedition to tackle the Ellsworth Mountain range in Antarctica. Tall and lean, with red hair, he struck me as an older version of Richie Cunningham from the old TV show, "Happy Days."
- **Celia Martin,** 45, Bill's sister, also an orthodontist from Gainesville. She was the only woman on the trip. Like her brother, she was lean and athletic. She turned out to be tougher than some of the guys on our crew.
- **Corwin "Corky" Peterson,** 69, a retired data processor from Minneapolis. Like me, Peterson had dreamed of travelling to the North Pole since he was a boy. He turned out to be a strong skier, one of the strongest in our group. He reminded me of Grandpa Walton.
- **Paul Pfau,** 49, a deputy district attorney for the Los Angeles DA's office. Pfau had led successful expeditions to Mt. Everest. Quiet and reserved, he told me once we were on the ice that his experiences at Everest were not nearly as gruelling   as our quest for the pole would prove to be.
- **Mike Warren,** another Gainesville resident, one who had done well as a commercial real estate developer. He had scaled Mt. Rainier and trekked to the top of Kala Patar in the Nepalese Himalayas. Close your eyes when he was talking, and you'd swear you were hearing Woody Allen. While the rest of us broke camp each day on the ice, he was busy packing his rucksack. He made an art form of it. He was a particularly shrill whiner.
- **Doug Hall, 40,** of Cincinnati, Ohio, founder of Richard Saunders International and the Eureka Ranch, a think tank that develops new product ideas for such corporations as Nike, Disney, AT&T, American Express and Coca-Cola. Hall was a marketing guy, and he marketed our expedition to the hilt. He landed a dozen big-name corporate sponsors and had their logos stitched to our parkas. He also created the charity around which our expedition revolved.
- **Randy Swanson,** 42, owned an auto repair shop in Grandville, Michigan. He had travelled to Africa to climb Mt. Cameroon and Australia to scale Mt. Bartle-Frere. He also was on Schurke's Ellesmere Island trek in 1997. A stalwart fellow, amiable and clever, Swanson was the opposite of a flashy self-promoter – the kind of guy you'd want in your corner. With his drooping

moustache, he bore a striking resemblance to Adm. Robert Peary, although Swanson was a bit stockier.

- **Craig Kurz,** 37, of Cincinnati, Ohio. Kurz was CEO of The HoneyBaked Ham Co., a runner, scuba diver, white water rafter and cross-country and downhill skier. Maybe five-four, maybe 135 pounds, Kurz was, at least physically, the smallest person on the trip. But he was as strong as any of us and, like Randy, a total team player. The first time I saw Kurz was that December in Minnesota. He was wearing shorts.
- **David Golibersuch,** 56, part of the General Electric research and development team in Schenectady, N.Y. He considered himself a novice mountaineer. The stories he told quite often seemed to have no end – and no point. But by the time our journey together was ended, he would perhaps learn the most valuable lesson of any member of our team.

Schurke's purpose in calling us together for the training session was two-fold. The first was to subject team members to Arctic-like conditions so they could see if the trip was something they truly wanted to take on.

The second was to give Schurke and Bill Martin, our expedition co-leader, a sense of whether the Arctic rookies could stand up to the rigours of the trip. I felt confident I was up to the task. I knew I could stand to get a wee bit more fit, but I also knew I could do it.

That first night, most of the members of our team talked about how they'd taken stock of their lives around the age of 40 and that they felt an inexplicable yearning to take on significant physical challenges, like climbing mountains, exploring wildernesses, going where few had dared to go. With the exception of Corky Peterson, it almost seemed as if each of them were dealing with a mid-life crisis – or if not a crisis, a come-to-reckoning phase of their lives.

For me, this trip was the realisation of a childhood dream.

It was a great escape for the children of the '70s in Northern Ireland whenever it snowed – a welcome diversion from the realities of the war zone that Belfast and all of Northern Ireland had become.

I was 11 the first time I saw a car bomb explode in my hometown of Lisburn. The television news had aired an account of the discovery of a "suspect device" in the form of a car loaded with explosives parked at the town centre. A tip had come in that the device had a 30-minute timer.

Without our parents knowing, my brother, Bill, and I hopped on our bikes and cycled up to the town centre. It was getting dark, and the security forces had cleared a crowd of on-lookers back to a safe distance of about 500 yards or so.

We watched with excitement, as we would have had we been waiting for a fireworks display. Suddenly the car erupted it a bright orange flash, followed by a huge FA-BOOM. I felt the concussion in my chest.

As children, we had little understanding of the implications of what we had seen. Years later, in conversations with friends my age who grew up in other countries, we would occasionally find ourselves talking about our childhood fears. They would talk of monsters and ghosts and imaginary creatures that went bump in the night. The demons haunting my nightmares were men in black ski masks who carried guns – and they were all too real.

Against that backdrop, a fresh snowfall made the world seem fresh and clean. It helped us forget, if only for a short time, "the Troubles."

Our first morning on the ice of White Iron Lake, the temperature was 10 degrees. Schurke shared three facts with us. One, water takes heat away from your body 25 times more rapidly than air. Staying warm means staying dry. Two,

Ellesmere the dog

one in four people on treks in the high Arctic fall through the ice into the water. Three, if you fall in, you have about 10 minutes to get out or you're a goner.

I should note here that I may have had a bit of an advantage over my teammates in terms of my ability to endure the cold. As a child, my two brothers and I slept in a large double bed. Our home had no central heating, and when we awoke on winter mornings, a thick layer of frost would have formed on the inside of our bedroom window.

As the youngest and smallest, I slept in the middle. During the night, my brothers would turn and wrap themselves in the covers. This had the unhappy result of stretching the covers tight, several inches above me. I had plenty of cold air circulating between the blanket and my epidermis. In this way, I was conditioned to tolerate chilly conditions.

That morning was the first time Paul's dogs had been out for a run since the previous winter. He instructed us to run chains under the sled runners in an effort to slow the dogs down. Due to a lack of snow, Paul directed us out onto White Iron Lake, just down the hill from his lodge. On the ice of the lake, chains or no chains, the sled runners might as well have been greased with butter.

The dogs pulled too quickly to be safe considering the weight of the sleds. At that speed, it would be too easy to be pinned against a tree and snap a few ribs. Or glance off the tip of a rock and flip a sled, with similar results.

Early one morning, we were awakened by Paul's hollering that the ice was cracking and we had 30 minutes to break camp, pack our gear and skedaddle. This was an unannounced drill to prepare us for the possibility of breaking ice on the way to the Pole.

Icy Moonscape

Thirty-two minutes later, we were off and running – two sleds and 16 dogs, with all our gear packed and tied down on the sleds. In that moment, it felt that the team was coming together. It was a very good feeling.

Once camp was set, we learned about celestial navigation. Each of us had a turn with the sextant, sighting along the sun and the noon meridian. Today, a hand-held Global Positioning System makes compasses and sextants obsolete, until your last batteries die. Before the GPS, one was forced to rely on one's resourcefulness. The notion of navigating by the stars had far more appeal for me.

At the end of our training session, we were ordered to strap on our gear and go down to the lake. There, we received further instructions to ski straightaway into a hole in the ice that Schurke had obligingly chopped open for yet another drill.

Swanson was the first of us into the drink. He extricated himself fairly gracefully. A dissatisfied Schurke looked for a spot where the water would be deeper. A few hundred yards to the leeward, he spotted a black hole and had us follow him there.

I looked to see where the ice was thinnest at the edge of the hole and skied toward it. My idea was to get rid of as much of the thinnest ice as possible, which would hopefully make my getting out easier. The ice cracked and in I went, completely submerged. My skis came off, although they quickly floated to the top.

I remember the sudden shooting pains of cold and shock. My breath was completely taken away. At the same time, I knew I would be pulled out if I got into trouble. But if ever there were a time when I didn't fool around, that was it. I grabbed the business end of my ski poles and used them as ice picks to pull myself, as Schurke had taught me a couple years earlier.

I felt significantly colder the instant I was out of the water. With an air temperature of 15 degrees below zero Celsius, the water was much warmer at zero. I hustled 200 yards back to the sauna next to the lodge, sopping wet.

Sprinting, I remember thinking that warmth was only seconds away here in Minnesota, knowing I'd experience it momentarily. Should I fall into the ice of the Arctic Ocean on the way to the North Pole, that same comfort would be unavailable for a thousand miles in any direction. There would, of course, be no sauna in the Arctic.

But I was drawn from my childhood to see what was there. I recently ran across these words from "Arctic Dreams" by Florian Schulz. They captured my feelings from those early days:

"When I dreamed of the Arctic in the past, it was the thoughts of a vast unspoiled wilderness filled with resilient life; a landscape so unknown and so big my imagination could run free creating a fascinating sense of wonder and desire to explore. As wilderness is shrinking around the world, we need such wilderness ... We need it to simply give our mind and spirit the freedom to roam!"

Castle Street, Lisburn, 1963 - my first winter.

"Men wanted for hazard-
es, bitter cold, long mon-
constant danger, safe retu-
recognition in case of suc-

"Men wanted for hazardous journey. Small wages, bitter cold, long months of complete darkness, constant danger, safe return doubtful. Honor and recognition in case of success."

Ernest Shackleton,
from a newspaper advertisement for his Endurance expedition

Chapter 3

FROM EDMONTON

Our itinerary called for the team members to meet in the Alberta city of Edmonton to review last-minute plans and make sure the gear was in working order and ready to go. We also were told to be prepared to submit to interviews and videotaping with all sorts of news media.

That finished, we would fly to Resolute, a small Inuit village of about 150 people and the world's northernmost outpost with regularly scheduled air service.

From there, we would be flown 800 miles north – dogs, sleds and all –and dropped off on the ice.

I knew that everyone on the team had gotten Platinum American Express cards, which offered its holders the privilege of free medical evacuation from anywhere in the world. For this, they had paid $300 apiece.

I was fortunate to come across a less expensive option. On my way to Edmonton, I still had no provision for emergency evacuation, should it prove necessary. My flight took me through Amsterdam. At the airport there, I spied a kiosk with an offer for medical evacuation insurance for 45 Euros, or about $60.

I spoke to the salesman and asked if the policy was effective anywhere on the planet. He said it was. I asked if I could have that in writing. He assured me that the terms of the policy clearly spelled out "anywhere in the world." So I signed up for the policy and gave the guy my money.

"Oh, by the way," the salesman said. "Might I ask where you're going?"

Sure, I said. "The North Pole."

His jaw dropped, but he quickly collected himself.

"Oh well, I guess it would be great publicity for our company."

I was the first of our gang to arrive at the hotel in Edmonton, a day ahead of schedule. I was coming the greatest distance, passing through more time zones than any of the other team members, so I wanted to give myself adequate time to shake off the effects of jet lag.

Next to arrive were the dogs. They came in cages in the back of two pickup trucks driven by a pair of Schurke's employees all the way from Ely, Minn., a distance of more than 1,000 miles.

By the end of my second day there, the members of the Aspiration Expedition had all arrived. The whole idea of calling it the Aspirations Expedition in the first place was something one of our Cincinnati teammates, Doug Hall, had come up with. He'd created a charity he was calling Great Aspirations, the idea being to help children

An encounter with Brian Blessed at Resolute Bay

achieve in school. Who could be opposed to such a thing?

Think of Hall as a modern-day P.T. Barnum, and you won't be far off. He sold the concept of the Aspirations Expedition to a dozen or so major corporations – among them, Johnson & Johnson, Pringles, the M&M candy company, Nesquik, landing sizeable sponsorships from each in the process.

In return, Hall had patches embroidered with the corporate logos of each sponsor stitched to red anoraks that he had made up for us. More accurately, he gave us the option if we wanted the patches or not.

My thinking was, well, why not. One team member, Randy Swanson, decided he'd rather not have them. From that point, Hall was rather frosty toward Swanson. I needled him a bit myself, calling him to his face more than once, but with a wink, "an uncharitable bastard."

Hall had hired the aptly named Bragman, Nyman and Cafarelli, a public relations firm with offices in New York and Beverly Hills, to beat the publicity drum for the expedition and Hall's charity. The agent assigned to us, John Paul Buchmeyer, had marching orders to drag whatever media he could to Edmonton.

Buchmeyer was under instructions from Hall to work the telephone like a monkey on methamphetamine, spreading the message about our North Pole expedition and how we were doing it to inspire kids to do better in school and how you could follow our progress on the aspirationsexpedition.com website Hall had created, and on and on. Hall had even managed to enlist the support of Tom Wilson, creator of the funny pages character, Ziggy, to chronicle our progress in his syndicated comic strip.

Under Hall's master plan, a big part of what we were supposed to be doing in Edmonton was getting video of the team mushing through the snow, as if we were actually en route to the pole – which, I suppose, we were. In a way.

Unfortunately, no one had thought to call ahead to see if there actually was snow in Edmonton. As it happened, there wasn't. The resourceful Buchmeyer managed to locate a ski slope several miles from town where they had a snow machine. We donned our gear, piled the dogs into several vans and drove there.

It was not much of a slope. From the distance, it resembled a pimple on the horizon, although a white pimple. Hall rubbed his hands together in anticipation.

When we got there, Schurke asked me to harness some dogs to a sled and get them running around for the cameras. I did so, and then headed the team for a snow-covered area without realising it was a restricted area.

I'd gone about 200 metres when I heard the muffled sound of something running in the snow behind me. I turned my head and, to my horror, saw a pair of massive black rottweilers hot on my heels. Evidently, these dogs patrolled this area and, in the hubbub, no one had thought to lock them up.

My first thought was that they were chasing my dogs – and that, as big as they were, the rottweilers would be no match for a pack of Inuit huskies. But to my surprise, they weren't at all interested in the dogs – it was me they were after. I remember thinking I'd come all this way imagining that my greatest danger would be polar bears, only to end up being mauled by two bloody rottweilers.

So there I was, riding along in full view of a half dozen video crews, kicking and thrashing at these slobbering, snarling monsters. Kurz later suggested that the footage would help fill up an Aspirations Expedition blooper reel, which Hall could conceivably market on the Home Shopping Network.

At any rate, my dogs finally realised what was happening. They turned the sled around, lunged after the rottweilers and, in a moment, had the brutes running off with their stubby tails between their legs.

That evening, we reviewed several emergency procedures, including what to do in case we were attacked by a polar bear. Schurke had brought along a .308-caliber hunting rifle and a 20-gauge pump-action shotgun.

The latter was loaded with six shells designed to create three distinct effects, each progressively more desperate. The first two were called "crackers." They were packed with load that would explode at about 100 yards, creating a bright flash and a loud bang that, hopefully, would scare off any approaching polar bears without injury. The second shells were rubber bullets that would smart but cause no permanent damage. The two shells that would be the last to be fired each contained a lead slug.

We all listened intently as Schurke explained that he would have the .308 trained on any encroaching bear while I would ply the shotgun against it. Should the shotgun prove ineffective once all six rounds had been fired off, Schurke would then use the .308 and aim to fire a killing shot. In any case, our goal would be to protect us while inflicting the least possible harm to the bear.

That night, I was awakened from a deep sleep with the phone ringing. Reaching for the phone in a groggy stupor, I held it to my ear and heard a curt, authoritative-sounding male voice utter these words:

"Mr. Humphries? Edmonton police here. We have a 14-year-old girl in the reception of the hotel who says she spent the night in your room. We have laws against that sort of thing, sir."

I went into a momentary panic before I realised the voice belonged to Bill Martin, cracking his idea of a joke. He received a few expletives for his trouble. I think I laid awake the rest of the night.

The next morning, I walked into the hotel restaurant to get a bit of breakfast and sitting there was the British actor Brian Blessed. It turned out he was on his way to the magnetic North Pole, on his first polar trek. I joined him for breakfast, and we talked about our respective adventures.

Given his high profile in the UK, I wondered if he were able to travel much without being recognised. He told a story about being on the summit of one of the lesser mountains in Nepal. Coming up the other side was a Chilean expedition.

As they reached the top, the leader doffed his goggles and said to him, "Flash Gordon's alive," which happened to be one of the actor's more memorable lines from the film "Flash Gordon."

And then, almost before I knew it, it was time to pack the dogs and our gear on the plane for the next leg of our journey, to the Inuit village of Resolute. In Edmonton, we were still in the civilized world. Once we arrived in Resolute, we would have crossed into the frontier.

The cold earth slept below,
Above the cold sky shone;
And all around,
With a chilling sound,
From caves of ice and fields of snow
The breath of night like death did flow

The cold earth slept below;
Above the cold sky shone;
And all around,
With a chilling sound,
From caves of ice and fields of snow
The breath of night like death did flow...

Percy Bysshe Shelley

Chapter 4

AS FAR NORTH AS CIVILIZATION GOES

It's a neat bit of irony that the town's name rhymes with "desolate." Resolute is about 1,000 miles from the nearest tree on one side, and that far again – 1,048 miles, to be exact – from the North Pole on the other. It is also one of the coldest inhabited places in the world, with an average yearly temperature of minus 16.4 degrees Celsius or about 2 degrees Fahrenheit. The roads and most of the terrain are all gravel.

It's a village of some 185 Inuit people who live primarily in prefabricated dwellings that look like corrugated metal cylinders laid sideways and half buried in the snow.

Many of the dwellings had propped up against them a polar bear hide stretched out on a wooden frame to dry outside or a frozen seal carcass laying in the snow. Or both. Once a day, the woman of the house would step outside with a hatchet. She'd chop off a piece of seal, carry it back inside and cook it, usually by frying or boiling. I'm told seal tastes like fishy beef, but I never tried it – largely owing to that description.

Resolute has a co-op store, where you can buy musk ox jerky, snowmobile parts, nails, toilet paper and aspirin, among other items. Oddly enough, considering its size, the town also has two hotels. They compete quite vigorously, though, since Resolute is a point of departure for explorers, adventurers, mining expeditions, hunting or research, to name a few examples. Our base of operations, where Wecker, our base camp manager would be lodged for the next two to three weeks, was the Southcamp Inn.

The town also was home base for a Royal Canadian Mounted Police station that covered a territory of roughly half a million square miles in the then-newly created Canadian province of Nunavut. The station was manned by exactly two

Bill Martin dog walking Arctic style

Mounties, both of whom were exceedingly glad to have our company, if only for a short time.

Indeed, they seemed almost starved for company from the outside world, as if they had endured an unbearably long stretch of solitary confinement. After extended periods in such a remote part of the world, surrounded by the same Inuit faces week in and week out, they were only too happy to strike up an acquaintance with someone fresh. And so they were happy to accommodate any need Wecker might have. The following story is one example.

While the rest of the Aspirations Expedition was slogging to the Pole, through the most punishing conditions imaginable, Wecker was snug as a bug at the South Camp Inn with time on his hands. One sunny sub-zero day, to satisfy his journalistic curiosity, he borrowed the inn's van and headed out into the frozen countryside. The road became increasingly less visible the farther he went, until he became stuck in snow halfway up the van's hubcaps a few miles outside town. In a matter of moments, the sheer cold turned the snow to ice, effectively locking all four wheels into place. The engine would start, but the wheels wouldn't turn.

Fortunately for Wecker, Resolute Bay is surrounded by a huge track – the locals call it "the ice road" – that German drivers in the employ of Audi and Volkswagen use to torture-test various vehicles. Working in shifts, the Germans tested vehicles on the ice road 24 hours a day, seven days a week. Wecker flagged down a German at the wheel of one of the early Audi TT's and hooked a ride to the Mounted Police station.

When he arrived at the station, both Mounties were on duty. They sprang to attention. Would you like a cup of tea to take the edge off the cold? they wanted to know. Some fresh biscuits? Is there anything we could do for you, eh, anything at all?

Well, yes, Wecker said. He explained the situation. The red-jacketed gendarmes quickly pulled on their snow gear, started up their Chevrolet Suburban with the Royal Canadian Mounted Police shields on the driver and passenger doors and assured Wecker they'd have him unstuck in no time. After the Suburban had idled for 10 minutes to warm up, the three of them drove off to where the South Camp van was locked into the ice.

One of the Mounties pulled a huge logging chain from the back of the Suburban. One end, he hooked to the Suburban's front bumper; the other, to the van's rear bumper. He took a few steps backward.

"OK, let 'er rip," he said to the Mountie behind the wheel of the Suburban.

Wecker expected the Mountie who was driving to move slowly in reverse to take up the slack in the chain. Instead, he stomped the accelerator to the floor. Wecker was flabbergasted. The suburban lurched to a stop when the chain went taut. Instead of stopping, the Mountie crept forward a few feet, shifted back into reverse and repeated the procedure, three times in rapid succession – WHAM, WHAM, WHAM!

The Suburban's front bumper flew off. Without hesitating, the other Mountie unhooked the chain from the detached bumper, pulled it under the Suburban and hooked it onto the frame.

"This is gonna be tougher than I thought, eh," said the Mountie behind the wheel. The other Mountie took a few steps back and gave him the thumbs up. Once again, the Suburban bucked into reverse, taking the slack out of the chain in a second, coming to a bone-jarring halt. This happened maybe three times – WHAM, WHAM, WHAM! – until the bumper of the South Camp Inn van ripped away.

This time, the Mountie with the chain connected it to the van's frame. With a few more lurches, the van was pulled free. The detached bumpers were stashed into their respective vehicles. The Mounties told Wecker not to worry, that the people at the South Camp Inn would understand. The only way to get a truck or a car of any kind unstuck in the Arctic ice is to jerk it out. There's nothing slow and easy about it. Everybody up here knows that, they assured Wecker.

"Make sure you come and see us while you're in Resolute – we'd be glad to show you around," the Mounties told Wecker as they headed back to town.

Wecker felt badly about the van, but the Mounties had been right in their assessment. Aziz Kheraj showed no sign of being the least bit irritated about having to weld the bumper back onto the van, saying he'd have one of his men take care of it the next day.

Aziz was owner/operator of the South Camp Inn. He was a Tanzanian ex-patriot known by everyone in these parts as Ozzie. The circumstances that caused him to leave Tanzania for Resolute Bay were somewhat murky, but he was a friendly, gracious host. His wife, an Inuit woman named Aleeasuk Idlout, was reputed to be the most skilled polar bear hunter and hunt guide in that part of the world.

As for the inn, it was clean, homey and quite comfortable, especially given its frontier outpost location. A tureen of hot soup was on the burner 24 hours a day, as was the coffee pot. If Randy Reid, the cook, wasn't on duty, you could always go into the kitchen and help yourself, as long as you cleaned up afterward.

The scene there was reminiscent of the bar from the original "Star Wars," the one where Han Solo rubs elbows with beings from the far corners of the universe. Given Resolute's standing as the northernmost point on the planet with regularly scheduled jet service and a point of departure for Arctic expeditions, it draws all kinds of intriguing characters from all kinds of places.

I reconnected with Brian Blessed there, for example. At one point, the three-day forecast for the greater metropolitan Resolute area was calling for minus-20-degree temperatures, with winds up to 50 mph. Blessed was not pleased.

''I can't imagine any bloody worse news than that!" he said in his booming stage voice to his assistant, Gilles Kershaw.

If you happened to be planning to take a flight from here to Bathurst Island as Blessed was, then pull a fibreglass sled some 100 miles beyond that to the magnetic North Pole, it was bad news indeed. Still, he intended to push on, blizzard or not.

At 62, Blessed was a bearded, thick-bodied bear of a man with a penetrating gaze and a basso profundo Shakespearean voice. He was also an international film actor. The son of a Yorkshire coal miner, he played the ghost in Kenneth Branagh's

David Wecker base camp
manager

"Hamlet," Caesar Augustus in the BBC production of "I, Claudius" and Voltan, king of the Hawkmen, in "Flash Gordon." He was often cast as a king. He carried himself like one as well.

One of our team members asked him why in the world a person would want to drag a sled to the magnetic North Pole.

"Because I think the greatest danger in life is not to take the adventure. Too many of us arm ourselves with insurance policies. Too many of us are dying slowly, measuring out our lives in teaspoons, as the poet once said."

With that, he launched into a story about George Lee Mallory, whom he portrayed in the 1990 film, "Galahad of Everest," based on Mallory's 1924 assault on Mt. Everest, his second attempt to scale the world's tallest peak.

"By 1919, the North and South poles had been discovered – Everest was the third pole," Blessed said.

"There was a poetry to Mallory's climbing, an artistry and gallantry with which he moved. He was known as the Galahad of Everest. On his first expedition, in 1920, he climbed to 20,000 feet.

"On his second trip, at the age of 35, climbing with a man named Andrew Irving, he made it to 28,000 feet without oxygen – an amazing achievement.

"They were backed by a man named O'Dell. One man. Imagine! O'Dell climbed to 25,000 feet, then to 27,000. Then the mist cleared, and he looked up. And there, far above him, were two figures so small they looked like ants, still climbing: Mallory and Irving.

"And that was the last anyone saw of them. Just as Sir Galahad died when he drank from the chalice, Mallory died when he touched the summit."

Irving's body has never been found, although Mallory's body was recovered in 2000. Until that discovery, the story was one of the great mysteries of the expedition world.

"And a mystery is a rare commodity these days," Blessed said.

"If by some odd chance we had discovered Mallory's remains when we were making the film, I would have covered them to keep the mystery intact."

Three years after the movie, Brian says, he returned to climb Everest in earnest. He got to 28,250 feet without an oxygen mask. He would have climbed farther, he says, but he had to help a fellow team member back down. He intended to try again the following spring.

He was expecting his trip to the magnetic North Pole to take 12 days.

"I'd prefer to take longer – I think I love exploring more than acting," he said. Then, dropping his voice a register for maximum effect, he paraphrased T.S. Eliot:

"We shall not cease our exploration. And the end of our exploring will be to arrive at the place where we started and to know it for the first time."

Some years later, I learned I had a personal connection to Mallory. Together with my grandfathers, William Watson and George Humphries, he had fought the Germans at the Battle of the Somme on the western front during World War I, as had Belfast native C.S. Lewis.

The battle lasted from the first of July to Nov. 18, 1916, during which time, some 1,500,000 men lost their lives. Even today, 60,000 tons of bullets, shells and other metal ordnance are extracted from the fields in the Somme region. It's called "The Metal Harvest." The battle was particularly poignant for those of us in Northern Ireland because the Ulster division of the British army suffered 5,500 casualties the first morning alone.

Both of my grandfathers were part of the Ulster Division. My paternal grandfather went over the top, up and out of the trenches at 7:30 the first morning of the battle. My mother's father was a gunner in the Royal artillery in the same division as George Mallory.

In the summer of 2009, I travelled to the Somme battlefields with my brother, Brian. We wanted to walk in the footsteps of both our grandfathers, to perhaps get a sense of what they had experienced – or at least to stand on that same ground. I don't know how to describe what an emotional few days it was for both my brother and myself.

Both grandfathers survived. Both returned home, married and raised families, although neither ever talked about the battle with their wives or their children. Their narratives skipped a generation, to their grandchildren.

I was quite young, so I don't recall much of what they had to tell about it, only that it was the most horrible experience of their lives. What I do remember is that my Grandfather Humphries was in a weakened state by that point in his life, the result of the residual effects of the mustard gas and shell shock he was exposed to all those years ago.

One day that April, a Twin Otter flew a load of produce to Grise Fiord on Ellesmere Island, about 150 miles from Resolute, up the Barrow Strait to the northeast. On the return flight, the plane was carrying the Hamlet of Resolute municipal jackhammer.

Not quite 150 people live in Grise Fiord, and nearly all of them Inuit. The place was discovered in the previous century by Danish explorers. They observed that, when the icebergs in the bay rubbed up against one another, the sound was like pigs grunting. "Grise," in fact, is Danish for "pig."

Robert Sheaves, a one-time Newfoundlander who lives there with his Inuit wife and daughter and who balances the village's accounts, shared this information with our base camp manager, who Schurke and a few others of our team had taken to calling "Commander Dave." Sheaves also explained the reason the Hamlet of Grise Fiord borrowed the jackhammer from the Hamlet of Resolute.

One of the village's elders had died a short time earlier. His family asked to borrow the jackhammer so they could dig his grave. The permafrost in this part of the world starts at ground level and goes straight down at least 2,000 feet. And when a grave needs to be dug, even with a jackhammer, it takes a strong man three days to get the job done. That's as good an indication of how "cold" cold gets in this part of the world that I know of.

The Inuit people have not been in this part of the world very long. Where you and

I come from, they're often referred to as Eskimos. Someone other than them gave them that name a long time ago. The word translates to "raw-meat eater" in English. They prefer the name they gave themselves.

The Canadian government brought the first Inuit here from northern Quebec and Baffin Island in the early days of the Cold War. Dan Leaman, the senior administrative officer of Resolute Bay, has spent the past 20 years putting together a history of this town and the surrounding region.

He said the Inuit are believed to have come to the Western Hemisphere from Asia, across the frozen Bering Strait between Russia and Alaska sometime in the 1400s. From there, it's thought they moved east into the Canadian prairies and forests.

The first Inuit people in Resolute Bay were literally shipped here by the Canadian government in 1953. Six years earlier, when no one lived here, the Canadian and U.S. governments established a joint Arctic weather station here. That was followed in 1950 by the Royal Canadian Air Force and U.S. armed forces.

"There was an issue of sovereignty in those days," Leaman said.

"To establish sovereignty, you need to have people living there. And of course, everyone was afraid the Soviets would invade at any moment from the other side of the Pole. So it was important to establish Canadian sovereignty here."

The first 16 Inuit to come to Resolute comprised three families. They were accustomed to living off the land. But the game in northern Quebec and on Baffin Island where they lived had dwindled due to a string of especially hard winters. And the Canadian government painted a misleading picture of plenty of good hunting, fishing and trapping up north.

"It was quite a sales job they did on the Inuit," Leaman said.

"The government wanted to establish a civilian work force to support the military presence, both here and on Ellesmere. But they enticed the Inuit with stories about all the animals that were here to hunt.

"They were housed in extremely poor accommodations. And they came to call themselves 'relocatees.' It's one of the saddest chapters in Canada's history.

"Of course, when the Inuit arrived here, they became dissatisfied – this place was not the utopia they'd been told it was. They had to endure 24-hour darkness in the winter and 24 hours of sunlight in the summer.

"They were told that, if they didn't like it here, they could always go back to Quebec and Baffin. But when they asked to go back, the government wanted money to take them. Of course, they had no money. They were stuck."

So the Inuit adapted.

Eventually, they learned the region's beluga whale migration routes. They learned to hunt the polar bear and the narwhal. A second group of Inuit came here a couple years after the first. Their sons and daughters married and had children.

By the time of my visit, their grandchildren were buzzing around town on snowmobiles, listening to music on compact discs and leading wealthy hunters from Germany, Brazil and the United States on polar bear hunts. Resolute was limited to

37 bear kills a year – some of which the Inuit kept for themselves, some of which they allowed hunters from the outside world. At the time I was there, hunters were paying $20,000 each for the privilege.

The Inuit elders were concerned that the younger among them were losing their culture, speaking English better than the native Inuktituk language. But with the establishment on April 1, 1999, of the Canadian territory of Nunavut – the Inuit word for "our land" – they were hopeful they could begin to regain control of their destiny.

"This is our home now," said David Oingoot, who was a teenager when his parents brought him here to live.

"It was hard at first. But we learned. And now we have made this place our own."

Among the other intriguing characters we crossed paths with at the South Camp Inn was Raymond Mercredi. It had been two and a half years since he'd seen his mother in Yellowknife, two hours south of here by jet, on the north shore of Great Slave Lake. She was getting old, he said, and he wanted to see her while he still could.

Mercredi was a 43-year-old Cree Indian. He stopped in Resolute en route from his home at Grise Fiord. He had a job clearing ice and snow from the runway at the Grise Fiord Airport.

He was taking a stack of photographs to show to his mother. Among them were shots of Raymond and his friends skinning seals, musk ox and walruses. In the Arctic, everyone is a hunter.

A male walrus can weigh up to a ton, he said. A friend of his once was kayaking, hunting walruses, when he felt something bump his aluminum kayak. His friend didn't think anything of it, Raymond says, until he pulled his boat out of the water and found two holes, each as big around as his wrist, where a walrus had neatly perforated his hull with its tusks. Raymond said it took his friend two hours to stop shaking.

There was also a photograph of a team of Inuit natives pulling a narwhal from the water. Narwhals are small as whales go, only about 20 feet long. They have a single horn protruding, unicorn-style, from their skulls. Their horns can be almost as long as their bodies.

The water where the Inuit were pulling the narwhal onto the ice was red with its blood. Raymond said he was amazed at how much blood there was in that narwhal. That's why he took the picture.

Another photo was of a woman kneeling next to a polar bear she had shot. The woman was Raymond's wife. Her name was Mary, and she was the granddaughter of Robert Flaherty, famous in the 1920s and '30s as an Arctic filmmaker. It was Flaherty who made the film, "Nanook of the North." "Nanook" is the Inuit word for polar bear.

Where Raymond comes from, animals are not hunted for sport – at least not by the natives. The people there eat the meat from their kills, fashion clothing from the furs and hides and use the bones, antlers and tusks to make tools and carvings.

"We eat a lot of bear meat," he said. He spoke quietly, and his voice had a soft, almost musical quality.

"It is a good change from seal – which, if you've never had it, has a fishy taste. But you get used to it. Bear meat is tougher, with a taste all its own."

Normally, Raymond said, he gets the bear. But he told a story about a time the bear almost got him.

"I was attacked only one time by a polar bear. I think it was in March, seven years ago. I was out hunting, and I had a 6-point-5 Swedish Mauser military rifle. Which, if you know anything about rifles, holds four shells and has a bolt action. And I was using hard-point shells – soft points can ruin your hides. But I had only three shells in there.

"I seen a bear and was going to shoot it. I got to within 100 feet of him on my Skidoo. The first shot, I missed. That bear, he was running. The second shot, I thought I got him good. I seen him go down, and I waited a few minutes.

"Then I started to walk toward him. About 25 feet away, I was carrying a seal gaffe and threw it at him. He didn't move, so I walked to about 15 feet of him. That's when he got up and started coming after me.

"I had only the one shell left. But I hadn't ejected my second shell, so my gun wasn't ready to be fired again. I had no bullet in the chamber – only that empty shell. So I ran."

This drew chuckles from two other men at the next table. They could laugh because there he sat.

Raymond smiled, too, but only slightly. His eyes narrowed at the scene being played out in his memory.

"I didn't have time to jump on the Skidoo. Because when I looked back, he was maybe 10 feet behind me. I'm trying to get my rifle ready to shoot, and I looked behind me again. And the bear, he sat down.

"By that time, the rifle was ready. So I turned and shot him. And that was the shot that killed him."

Raymond lit a cigarette and took another sip from his coffee cup.

"I didn't think of it at the time I was skinning him on the ice," he said.

"But I had 50 or 60 miles to travel back to my home. That is a long time. And more than once, I had to stop, I was trembling so badly."

The view to the North atop Signal Hill overlooking Resolute is of a boundless white terrain that rolls on to the top of the world and down the other side. Turn around, and the view into the valley some 500 feet below is of five dozen prefabricated buildings clustered in a circle not quite a quarter-mile across.

In one of the larger buildings, the South Camp Inn, two of Ozzie's workers were passing the time late one morning that April watching Jerry Springer on the tube. Springer was setting up two men who were about to find out their girlfriends were lesbians.

"They're in for a surprise, eh?" said Keith Adams, the South Camp handyman.

"Heh heh heh," said Randy Reid, the inn's cook.

"Yeah, but I like Judge Judy better," Keith said.

"She's more straight-forward. Joe Wapner's the original, of course. But Judge Judy gives 'em hell."

Even here on the fringes of civilization, it's possible to enrich oneself with the benefits of modern culture. Then again, there's not much else in the way of entertainment. When they're done working, people shoot the breeze, eat, stay warm, sleep, smoke and drink coffee. They drink a lot of coffee.

If you want to apply for an alcohol permit and you're willing to wait two weeks, you can have a belt of the sweet nectar now and then, too – as long as you're also willing to pay to have it shipped here.

Throughout most of the so-called civilized world, people fear boredom. Here, they accept it. Boredom is relative. Take Rai Le Cotey, who had just arrived at the South Camp, his last stop before boarding a Twin Otter aeroplane for a two-and-a-half hour flight to a place called Eureka.

As dark as it gets

Among other "northernmost" points of interest, Eureka is the site of the world's northernmost ham radio station, maintained by the Canadian government to provide communications for its weather base here and a tank farm that holds 1.3 million gallons of diesel fuel to supply power for heat. The base has a year-round full-time minimum staff of eight, including the station program manager.

That was to be Cotey's job for the next three and a half months. He would work a shift at the Environment Canada office in Winnipeg, take a shift off with pay and put in a shift in the frozen north.

"When there's lots of sun, we have visitors and the new faces help," said Cotey, a 46-year-old bachelor.

"The hardest part is winter, when you have 24 hours of darkness a day. When you wake up, it's dark. When you have lunch, it's dark. And you don't want to go outside, because it's 50 below. Winter's the most depressing time. It's just flat-out bleak. Some handle it. Some stay in their rooms."

Cotey told how he spent a good deal of introspective time in his room during his tours to Eureka. After seeing the same people day in and day out, he said, you grow weary of them. So you go to your room.

"This year, we're supposed to get a couple more TV channels," he said.

"My last rotation, all we got was the CBC. Also, we have an extensive video library. Some of the favourites are 'Mars Attacks' and that one with Kurt Russell, 'The Thing.'

"It's about a small group of people stranded in an Antarctic weather centre and a monster that comes out of the ice to terrorize them. We sort of make comparisons to our situation and laugh."

At that, Cotey chuckled. His chuckle grew into laughter, and he laughed for a good 15 seconds, until he was laughing loudly. Then he abruptly stopped.

"Or you can surf the net," he said.

"Of course, I'm working on my computer all day long. So I don't find it relaxing to go back to the computer after spending eight hours staring at it. There's ping-pong, but nobody uses it.

"Occasionally, some of us will get together for a game of pool or darts or cards. But you get tired of that after a while."

Cotey patted his ample stomach and admitted that the Eureka staff did a fair amount of eating. Produce was flown in every three weeks, he said. In general, he said, the food is good, depending on the cook's mood.

Being from the big city of Winnipeg, Cotey was accustomed to more in the way of mental stimulation than he was getting in Eureka. Not that his job didn't keep him busy – the lights on the landing strip might go out, for instance, and he would have to see to it they got fixed. Or the generators might go out. If they aren't repaired in six hours, the station freezes. If they aren't repaired in 24 hours, he would order the base evacuated.

"You can learn to ignore boredom," he said.

"You can absorb yourself in your work. But all work and no play gets to you, too."

That's why Cotey always made sure he was equipped for his Eureka rotation. He said the Canadian government doesn't like him to talk about it.

"But the truth's the truth. I take a snort now and then. I do. Up here, you need something."

Which way to Belfast?

The land looks like a fairytale.

Roald Amundsen
Polar Explorer, circa 1911

Great God! This is an awful place!

Robert Falcon Scott
Polar Explorer, circa 1911

Chapter 5

FIRST NIGHT ON THE ICE

With the team freshly dropped off on the ice, watching the two Twin Otter aeroplanes that had minutes ago dropped us there disappear in the distance, we were reeling from the initial impact of the sheer cold. We were literally in shock, enveloped in coldness that was bone-chilling, mind-numbing, stark, sheer, painful, bitter cold. It was so cold that cold was all we could think about. It was a cold that was truly frightening.

And we had no place to go where we could get away from it.

At the same time, we were experiencing a collective sense of being miniscule specks in a vast icy wilderness. Our mood was anything but cheerful. More than one of us had thoughts very much along the lines of, "What in God's name have I gotten myself into?"

Straightaway, Schurke ordered us to harness the dogs to the sleds and get going. This was no environment to be standing around contemplating our navels. We knew the sooner we got moving, the sooner our bodies would generate warmth. And Schurke knew it better than any of us.

The plan was to head north for at least a few hours before making camp and hunkering down for our first night on the ice. We were roughly two weeks and 200 miles away from our destination if it were possible to travel there in a straight line. But given the obstacles we would face, we would have to cover many more miles to actually get there.

The temperature was pushing minus 30 Celsius. The winds were calm. For the most part, the early going was smooth, and the dogs were keen to pull.

After months of preparation and a lifetime of wanting to do this, it was a great feeling to finally be making my way toward my actual goal, not just rehearsing for it. Still, I felt more than a twinge of trepidation. Having gotten this far, I desperately wanted us to succeed. But there was no telling what kind of obstacles would present themselves. Still, for those first couple of hours, at least, everything went according to plan.

We slogged on, up and over two or three smaller pressure ridges about 10 feet high until we arrived at one that rose a more respectable 25 or so feet up from the ice.

Schurke decided it would be a good place to make camp our first night. With a good night's rest, team members and dogs alike would be fresh to attack the challenge. With the winds beginning to whip up, the pressure ridge also would offer a measure of shelter.

Sea ice landing

We began what would be our nightly ritual for the weeks to come. The dogs were unharnessed, clipped to a line and fed their daily rations of high-protein pellets. Soon after they had eaten, the dogs would curl up and go to sleep.

A large pot was filled with snow and placed on a propane burner to provide water for drinks. We mixed it with powdered apple juice, granulated orange juice and herbal tea to make steaming mugs that helped take the bite out of the cold.

We each looked after our assigned tasks. Mine was to tend to the dogs. Others pitched tents in the evening and took them down in the morning, and still others prepared hot drinks and meals.

One unusual piece of gear we had was key to getting those drinks ready for us as speedily as possible. It was the pot I mentioned a moment ago, a piece Hall designed and had custom-made for that purpose.

The pot was made of aluminum to distribute heat quickly and evenly, but its distinguishing factor was its bottom. Instead having a flat bottom, it was in the shape of a cone recessed up into the pot. The design diminished the pot's capacity, but it increased its efficiency in terms of its ability to melt snow in a hurry.

We took our meals in the cook tent, which also served as the sleeping quarters for our cooks, Hall and Kurz. We improvised seats in a circle by packing together snow and ice, then sat down for supper. That first night, the dinner consisted of pasta with some sort of spicy fat-based flavouring sprinkled from a shaker.

The dinner conversation that first night focused on what had transpired since that morning.

We'd departed from Resolute 14 hours earlier in two Ken Borek Air Ltd. Twin Otter aeroplanes. Twin Otters are 18-seaters powered by two jet engines that drive propellers. They set the standard for bush planes and are used around the world to fly in and out of difficult areas where landing space is limited. They're easily equipped with pontoons or skis, depending on the circumstances.

A Twin Otter carries about five hours of fuel. On a flight from Eureka to the Pole, Otters have to refuel at a wilderness fuel cache at 86 degrees north latitude in order to make it the Pole and back to the cache. There, they refuel again for the trip back to the Canadian weather base outpost at Eureka, where they have to refuel one final time to make the trip back to Resolute.

Because fuel considerations have to be taken into account on any flight to the pole, you can load up to – but no more than – 1,800 pounds of people and/or gear onto a Twin Otter. Each flight is literally calculated to the last pound. They can't be too heavy with either fuel or cargo, because they're landing on ice, using skis as landing gear, and it's difficult to know how thick the ice is at any given point or how much weight it can support. Planes have been known to break through the ice and sink into the black Arctic Ocean on such landings.

As noted, the Aspirations Expedition left Resolute in two Twin Otters. One carried eight of our team's members and their gear. Schurke and I piled into the other, along with Schurke's 18 dogs and his sleds.

Over dinner, I shared with the rest of the crew my impressions of the flight. My immediate observation was that it was intensely odiferous. For his part, Schurke worked on getting some sleep. So it was my responsibility to break up fights between the dogs, swatting at them with a club wrapped in foam rubber.

Dogfights erupted every 20 minutes or so. This breed of dog gives no warning when a scrap is going to break out, no prelude whatsoever – they go from zero to 60 in a second. Although they're quite passive around people, Inuit sled dogs are unusually aggressive toward one another. It's their nature to constantly challenge and provoke their own.

These fights were seldom between just two dogs – it was almost always three or four or five going at it at the same time. My job was to separate them as quickly as possible, before they could injure themselves and, in so doing, jeopardize the expedition. It was a worrisome task, considering the biggest among them weighed nearly 100 pounds.

I provided the dessert that first night. One of the agreements was that team members would take turns with dessert detail. I decided to get past that obligation right away and handed out Mars bars. That way, I wouldn't have to carry them in my pack any longer, and my burden would be that much lighter. The chocolate was rock hard from being in my pack all day.

We retreated to our tents, of which there were four, including the mess tent. I shared a tent with Swanson and Warren. I had plenty of experience sleeping in cold weather, so I had my "sleep system," as it's referred to in explorer circles, down pat.

Smooth running

Arctic road rage! Over taking can be hazardous as a dog being passed may take umbrage and start a fight

Essentially, I'd done it often enough and badly enough that I had figured out what not to do. My tent mates had not had the benefit of that experience.

For all intents and purposes, Swanson and Warren crawled fully clothed into their sleeping bags – wearing their long underwear, fleece tops and bottoms, socks, down booties, gloves and balaclavas. They looked like they were getting ready to rob a convenience store.

My sleeping garb consisted of my thermal underwear, nothing more. I climbed into my bag and kicked my legs for two or three minutes to generate body heat, which is the key to staying warm in the Arctic.

I would wake the next morning warm and toasty. Meanwhile, Swanson and Warren would sleep fitfully and awaken in cranky moods. Both developed a case of sleep envy, directed at me.

One other piece of gear for sleeping in the Arctic is an item generically known as the "pee bottle." It's a plastic one-litre container, and you take it into your sleeping bag with you. The idea is that, should you have to relieve yourself during the night, you can – without leaving the relative comfort of your sleeping bag.

Granted, it can be a bit of a trick making sure the lid is secured when you're finished, as you'll see in these pages later. But when handled responsibly, the pee bottle is a wonderful concept.

Here again, I seemed to have an advantage over my tent mates. I was able to perform this particular function while lying on my side. Unfortunately for Swanson and Warren, they were obliged to urinate from a kneeling position, which required them to expose a good part of their bodies to the frigid air.

Early on in the trip, in fact, when Swanson was in the process of doing just that, I heard him complaining.

"Why don't you stay in your sleeping bag?" I asked.

"I can't – it doesn't work unless I get up," he said.

Said I, "You should just lie on your side, like I do."

"What? How do you manage that?" he asked.

"I guess," I said, before rolling over and going back to sleep, "it depends on your equipment."

This is the Law of the Yukon, that only the Strong shall thrive;
That surely the Weak shall perish, and only the Fit survive.
Dissolute, damned and despairful, crippled and palsied and slain,
This is the Will of the Yukon, – Lo, how she makes it plain!

Robert Service

The Law of the Yukon

Chapter 6

AN IRISH HERITAGE OF EXPLORATION

The Aspirations crew was slow to shake off the effect of the cold our first morning on the ice. We got off to a chaotic start as we struggled in the freezing cold to get our respective acts together. The temperature was a nose-nipping 35 below. A 15-mile-an-hour wind made it feel that much colder.

Coming out of our sleeping bags, we were stiff and slow. We fumbled with tents and gear and with harnesses and dogs. Breakfast was a porridge-like glop sprinkled with more fat-based flavouring, coffee and a hot orange drink. It fell short of the standards of, say, the Ritz-Carlton. Nevertheless, it was delicious – hot and sweet.

Of all of us, Schurke was perhaps in the foulest mood. He called a meeting first thing and sternly called for a halt on the pagers. He was referring to the Motorola Iridium pagers each team member was carrying. These devices were tied into a global satellite communications system that enabled them to receive email messages from any point on the planet. Hall had generously provided each of us with a pager so we could stay in touch with friends and family members throughout our journey. The pagers would prove to be a huge encouragement factor, especially during the expedition's darkest hours.

It turned out Schurke had been awakened three times that first night by the sound of a beeping pager.

"Enough with the darn pagers when we're trying to sleep," he growled.

Good enough, we said – although we weren't doing a very good job of hiding our disappointment.

Minutes later, Schurke pulled his own Iridium pager from his pocket. He hadn't read the manual and asked one of the crew how to use it. He was surprised to discover he had four messages, including one from his 13-year-old daughter, Bria, with news she'd gotten straight A's on her report card. It was his own pager that had interrupted his sleep.

His face softened immediately. He checked his pager repeatedly from then on throughout each day. He also lifted the nighttime ban.

As we set out, we settled into a routine of stopping every hour on the hour for five minutes to re-hydrate and graze on a few handfuls of a mix of dried fruit, nuts and chocolate to replenish our energy. If needed, we would suck down a tube of Goo, a high-protein paste.

My role with the dogs involved walking alongside the sled, helping to push it up and over pressure ridges, guiding it through narrow passages in the ice. It was a seriously strenuous task. Fully packed, each sled weighed 1,200 pounds. With each passing day, of course, their weight diminished as food supplies were consumed, but the load was still heavy, cumbersome and awkward.

Arctic camping

I sustained my first injury coming down the backside of a pressure ridge. These are never smooth, slick, fast runs – the way is always uneven, bumpy and irregular, with huge slabs and splinters of rock-hard ice jutting this way and that – the kind of terrain that makes it all too easy to snap an ankle, dislocate a knee or tear a muscle.

I was straining to hold back the sled in an effort to keep it from coming down on top of the dogs when I lost my footing. My right knee slammed against a protruding chunk of cement-hard ice.

The pain was stunning. Almost immediately, my knee began to swell. That night and thereafter, the swelling increased to the point that I found it difficult to remove my wind layer pants. I asked Bill Martin, our wilderness medical expert, for his advice on the best way to treat the injury.

"Take some Ibuprofen," he said, adding with a smile, "and put some ice on it." I did, and it actually helped.

My first injury aside, we kept going. We had to – we'd taken too much time breaking camp. Schurke was keen on making up time we'd lost in the morning. For me, it was the first of many injuries to my legs that hampered my ability to work at full capacity. In fact, injuries became a daily routine for the team members working the sleds.

The person on sled duty is far more likely to be in harm's way than someone who is skiing along. Between the bulky sleds bouncing and careening down pressure ridges and trying to protect the dogs, injuries were part of the job. Later in the trip, we'd

Tom Crean

Ernest Shacklton

find a way to make it safer – but it took a few days and several painful mishaps to figure out.

That first injury brought home in a new way to me the harsh realities of travel in the high Arctic. I couldn't help but thinking of others of my countrymen who had explored desolate regions, both here and in the Antarctic; brave men who didn't have the advantages of modern technology I had – men like Tom Crean, Ernest Shackleton and Francis Crozier, a native of County Down, like myself.

Crean had a distinguished career from the end of the 19th century to the early 1920s, during what came to be known as the Heroic Age of Antarctic Exploration, a time in history when each expedition required endurance that tested men to their physical and mental limits. Crean was a member of three of the four main British treks to the South Pole.

As a boy, I would play out one of Crean's exploits in particular in the theatre of my mind. It happened during the Terra Nova Expedition of 1910-13, which embarked 168 miles from the South Pole. Crean was part of Robert Falcon Scott's final race to the South Pole. Eight men were on that trip. Too late, Scott realized he had provisions for only five. So he sent Crean and two others back across the Antarctic peninsula on foot to the base camp, located at a place called Hut Point some 750 miles away.

At one point, they faced the prospect of a three-day detour around a precipitous icefall. Running short on supplies, the three decided out of desperation to ride their sledge down the icefall, without any means of steering other than shifting their weight from one side to the other.

It must have been one hell of a ride. They slid nearly straight down for some 2,000 feet in a matter of seconds, narrowly missing vast crevasses, coming to a stop when the sledge flipped runners-up on an ice ridge. One of Crean's team, Lt. Edward Evans, would write later: "How we ever escaped entirely uninjured is beyond me to explain."

With more than 100 miles to go before reaching the safety of Hut Point, Evans was stricken with snow-blindness. Crean and the third man, William Lashly, began hauling Evans on the sledge, warming him with the last of their supply of brandy. They made it as far as a place called Corner Camp, some 30 miles from Hut Point. They had one or two days' rations left but five days still to reach Hut Point, and Crean's companions were suffering from scurvy. They had no choice but to stop.

It was decided Crean would continue on his own to bring back help. With a bit of chocolate and a few biscuits to sustain him, and no tent or survival gear, Crean marched 18 hours and collapsed on arrival at Hut Point. Days later, Lashly and Evans were both brought back to the base camp alive.

It is one of the most heroic and harrowing rescue tales of the Antarctic. Crean seemed a modest man to me, all the more admirable for it. In a rare written account, one of his letters offers this insight into his personality: "So it fell to my lot to do the 30 miles for help, and only a couple of biscuits and a stick of chocolate to do it. Well, sir, I was very weak when I reached the hut."

Crean also travelled with Shackleton in 1914 to the Antarctic on the storied expedition of the ill-fated Endurance. The goal of the Imperial Trans-Antarctic Expedition, as it was called, was to cross the continent from the bottom of the Atlantic to the bottom of the Pacific by way of the South Pole.

The ship was caught up in a drifting ice pack some six weeks after setting sail. Over the next nine months, it was slowly crushed. Shackleton ordered the crew to abandon ship and transfer the ship's supplies to the ice, where the crew set up camp.

They stayed there for two months, hoping their ice floe would drift toward Paulet Island, where they knew other explorers had stashed emergency supplies. It didn't. In April, their island of ice split apart, and Shackleton ordered his crew into the wooden lifeboats they had salvaged from the Endurance. Shackleton and his men drifted for five days before landing on Elephant Island. It was the first time in 497 days any of them had stood on solid ground.

Elephant Island was barren and remote, far from any shipping routes or hope of rescue. Shackleton decided to take the sturdiest of the lifeboats, christened James Caird after the expedition's main sponsor, and five crewmen, including Crean, and risk an attempt in an open boat across stormy seas to reach whaling stations at distant South Georgia, where they could find help.

Sixteen days later, after riding out hurricane-force winds that sank a 500-ton steamer bound for South Georgia from Buenos Aires, they landed their lifeboat on the island's unoccupied southern shore. Shackleton left three men there and, together with Crean and the fifth of their group, trekked continuously for 36 hours through uncharted mountains, somehow arriving at Stromness Whaling Station. Rescue parties were sent out immediately, one to bring back the three men from the southern shore and the other to Elephant Island, where the 22 crew members were found still alive.

It would be 39 years before anyone would successfully cross South Georgia; British explorer Duncan Carse in October 1955 travelled much the same route Shackleton had taken.

After he had completed the journey, Carse wrote: "I do not know how they did it, except that they had to – three men of the heroic age of Antarctic exploration with 50 feet of rope between them and a carpenter's adze."

In the preface to the book, "The Worst Journey in the World," one of Shackleton's associates, Apsley Cherry-Garrard offered this: " . . . if I am in the devil of a hole and want to get out of it, give me Shackleton every time."

Crozier preceded Crean and Shackleton by almost a century. He joined the British Navy in 1810 and made three Arctic voyages with Capt. W.E. Parry between 1821 and 1827. As second in command to James Clark Ross from 1838 to 1843, he explored the Antarctic and assumed command of John Franklin's Arctic expedition in 1847

Captain Francis Crozier

after Franklin perished in an attempt to find the Northwest Passage that went horribly wrong.

A statue of Crozier stands in the town Banbridge, about 10 miles from where I grew up. At each corner of the base of the statue is a polar bear. I remember thinking as a boy that the explorer was devoured by polar bears. I didn't learn until many years later that he froze to death after his ship, Terror, became stuck in the ice.

None of these men had global positioning systems, clothing made from high-tech fibres or any hope that, in an emergency, the knowledge they could always get on the radio and call for an air lift. What they did have was an abundance of grit, determination and resourcefulness.

I thought of how, as a child, I'd marvelled at what they were able to accomplish, against all odds. And now, here in the difficult circumstances and harsh surroundings of this desolate place, replete with modern advantages Crean, Shackleton and Crozier could never have imagined, my respect and admiration for them grew tremendously.

The Aspirations Expedition moved 11 miles closer to the pole on this day. Schurke seemed happy enough with that, considering we'd fumbled around until noon breaking camp, which gave us only about six hours of travel time. From this point on, we resolved to put in 12 hours each day on the ice.

Eskimo hunting principles was needing to use every bit that could be used ... after b and after every bit of no from the sea

Eskimo hunting principles were to
hunt only what was needed
and to use every part of the animal
that could be used ...
after being boiled and scraped,
and after every bit of nourishment
was removed from the seal,
the bones provided material for tools
and utensils.

... Anonymous polar traveler

Chapter 7

THE ULTIMATE
WEIGHT LOSS PLAN

If you're in shape, the ideal Arctic diet calls for an intake of 6,000 calories a day. If you're not in shape, stay at home. Arctic travellers, at the pace we were going and the cold we encountered, burn through nearly as many calories as a cyclist in the Tour de France, who typically would expend 7,000 calories during a race day. Under normal circumstances, the average male should consume 2,000 calories daily. The difference is that, in the harsh climes of the frozen north, your body has to burn more calories to stay warm. Stay warm, keep moving and stay alive – that's the deal when you're travelling in the Arctic Circle.

I guarantee that if you try this diet for two weeks – in conjunction with mushing across the frozen Arctic wilderness for 10 to 14 hours a day – you will lose weight like a sheep gets sheared, or your money back. After two-plus weeks of 6,000-calorie days on the slog to the Pole, I still managed to lose 20 pounds.

'Cook tent' the best part of the day

For the Aspirations Expedition, we aspired to a diet that contained loads of fat and, in addition to that, more fat. At the same time, meals can't be elaborate. They have to be prepared quickly, with a minimal expenditure of propane fuel.

In the Arctic, everything has to last until you get to where you're going. It's imperative to keep gear and supplies to a minimum in terms of weight, because the less energy you expend carrying stuff, the farther you can go. It's a simple principle.

Our menus looked like this:

- **Breakfast:** Instant coffee or herbal tea, made from boiling down snow, followed by a bowl of oatmeal/porridge, flavoured with a granular fat-based sweet flavouring. Hall commissioned a food scientist to develop a variety of sweet and savoury flavourings to make pack bland foods more appetising, at least minimally. Breakfast was one of two proper – and by that, I mean sit-down – meals each day.

- **Supper:** Hot Tang, a powdered orange drink available in the U.S. and popularized by astronauts on Gemini

Looking for a route through the ice rubble

missions in the mid-1960s, or herbal tea and instant coffee, followed by a bowl of pasta, again flavoured by a granular fat-based savoury flavouring. It might be lasagna flavouring, fried chicken flavouring, steak and onion flavouring or any of half a dozen others. This was the other sit-down meal.

Additionally, team members were expected to take turns providing dessert from their private stashes. These included Mars bars (thank you, Alan), as well as various other bars and chocolate treats. For the most part, each dessert was anxiously received. The one exception was the team member who distributed a handful of after-dinner peppermints pinched from a basket at the Southcamp Inn. (You know who you are.)

On top of that, we were instructed each morning to grab heaping handfuls of a mixture of Jolly Roger candies, chocolate chunks, cheese, nuts and dried fruit from a large plastic sack. This was for us to consume on our five-minute hourly breaks on the trail.

One other point: It is vital to maintain body hydration. In the harsh conditions of the far north, you can become dehydrated quickly. After all, your body is working at a fever pitch. A good way to tell if you have adequate fluid on board is if, when you urinate, the product is clear and colourless. If it's dark or too amber, you'd better get some water.

That's it in a nutshell. For your culinary enjoyment, I've included some authentic Inuit recipes here for the next time you find yourself travelling through the Arctic on your way to the North Pole. Note their simplicity. I can't vouch for them, but they are genuine Inuit recipes. And the Inuit people are after all experts on the subject. While these recipes may seem alien, possibly even bizarre to us, they are emblematic of the completely different world the Inuit people inhabit.

Ptarmigan

Take the feathers off the ptarmigan. Cut the meat and wash off dirt and feathers. Put in a pot with water and salt. Sometimes people make soup from it.

Bear Feet (or Ee-tee-yait')

Most people like the bear feet better than the meat. Boil the feet well, adding salt. Four feet require only about one teaspoon of salt. Take them out of the pot and let them cool. Eat them with seal oil.

Oogruk (or Bearded Seal) Flippers

Cut the flippers off the oogruk. Put the flippers in fresh blubber. Let them soak in blubber for about two weeks. Remove any loose fur. Then cut the feet into in small pieces and enjoy.

Seal Oil

Seal oil is made from the blubber or fat next to the skin of the seal. The blubber and skin is cut from the seal, sliced into strips and stored in seal pokes or tins. If left where warm or during the summer, it renders itself. From this, you have seal oil.

Seal Poke

This is not a dish for beginners. The inside of the seal, together with the head and all, is cut and taken out through the head part of the sealskin. The skin is then turned, cleaned and blown up for drying. This is then used to put the meats, berries, leaves, or other foods for storing in the winter. A good seal poke will last one, maybe two seasons.

Seal Head

Use a sharp knife to skin your seal. Remove the head and cut it into small pieces. If possible, dice the head. Pour the pieces into a pot of water and add salt. The original recipe says to "boil plenty good." When cooked, eat the meat. Break the skull and eat the inside of it, too, if you want.

Oogruk Intestine Soup

Wash the intestines carefully. Push the inside meat off the intestine with a spoon. Take the meat out of the intestine and wash again. Cook it in a pot with water. Cut blubber into little pieces and put them in a pot to boil. If you find yourself thinking, "Hey, this needs something," add salt.

The ice ridge was 30ft high

The wind goeth towards the south, and turneth about unto the north; it whirleth about continually, and the wind returneth again according to his circuits.

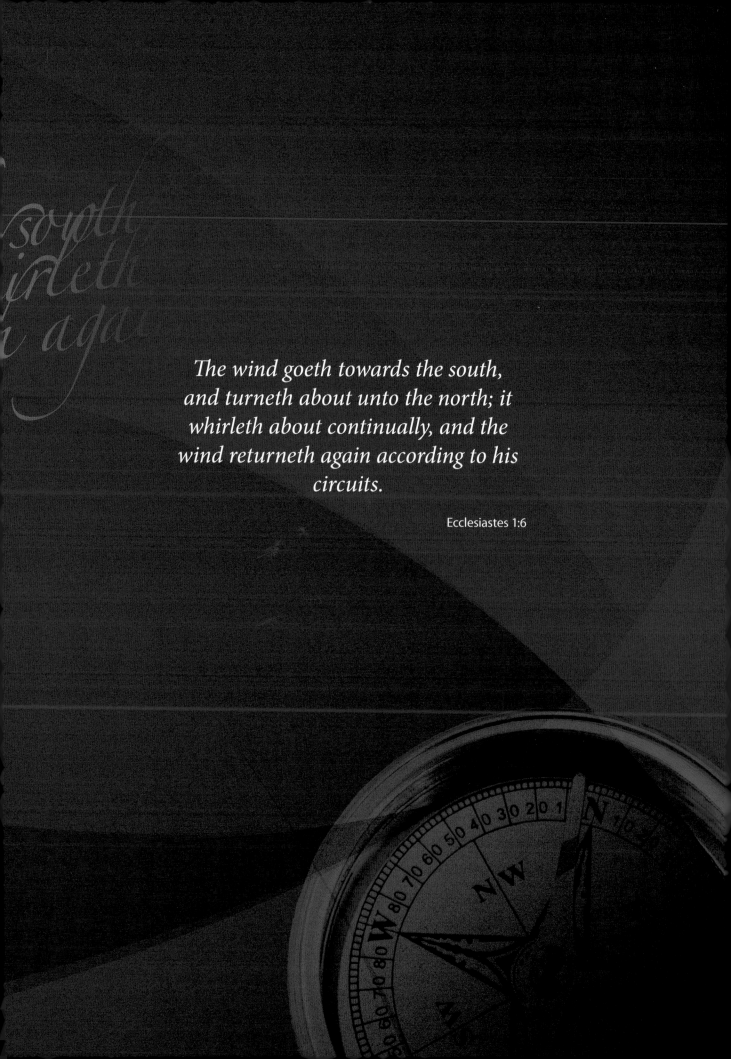

The wind goeth towards the south,
and turneth about unto the north; it
whirleth about continually, and the
wind returneth again according to his
circuits.

Ecclesiastes 1:6

Chapter 8

ARCTIC BAPTISM

The temperature was 44 degrees below zero the morning of the day when I experienced my first – and hopefully last – Arctic baptism.

The days had quickly grown progressively more gruelling. On this day, our third day on the ice, we'd covered perhaps 45 miles and still had another 155 to go before arriving at the pole.

When the going would get tough, Schurke kept us moving with this boot camp-style chant:

"How do you eat an elephant?" he would shout.

Which was our cue to shout in response:

"One bite at a time."

The farther we went, the more pressure ridges cropped up in our path. They seemed to be getting higher, too. At the same time, we weren't finding any frozen leads heading north.

Open water, one of the greatest dangers of the arctic"

A freshly frozen lead is ideal terrain for travelling in the high Arctic – the ice is new, which means it's smooth and flat. And it's pure ice, without layers of frozen snow to slow you down. Whenever we would come across a frozen lead, it was like clean sailing on a motorway. We could just go and go and go. We got to where we dreamed of finding frozen leads.

Another point about pressure ridges is that getting up and over them is never, ever a simple matter of shouldering the sled up a rise and down the other side. The path is strewn with blocks of rock-hard ice, as big as refrigerators, pianos, automobiles and houses, all pointing in every which direction, each presenting its own set of problems.

These blocks of ice can shift and move with the weight of the sleds, opening sudden holes that can swallow up legs, spring muscles and snap bones as if they were pencil leads. Or massive ice tables can come hurtling down at you, crushing you against other heavy slabs of ice.

Sometimes, we would hear the plates – or "pans" – of layered ice groan as they shifted and pushed, grinding one against the other. When an especially large pan suddenly snaps, it does so with a deep BOOM!, like a cannon going off in the distance, erupting in a ridge that can easily extend 10 miles or more.

From time to time, the upheaval of a pressure ridge would bring with it odd bits of debris. I remember coming across chunks of plastic and bottles, some inscribed with Russian Cyrillic writing, wondering what circuitous routes they had taken to get there.

The most strenuous part of a pressure ridge is muscling the sleds to the top. The way we did it was to pull back the main tug line that connected the dogs to the sled, giving the dogs two or three feet running space. Then we'd drop the line, holler "Hup!" to the dogs, and they would launch themselves tight into their harnesses.

At the same time, a couple of us would slam our shoulders into the back of the sled as if it were an American football tackle dummy. That might give us 12 inches of forward progress, or it might give us three or four feet. The whole time, it was a struggle to keep the sled from tipping.

In that herky-jerky fashion, with fits and starts, we'd make it to the top. It often took 20 to 30 minutes.

The descent down the other side was the more dangerous part. The sleds were, after all, 1,200-plus pounds fully loaded – almost as much as a grown rodeo bull. While we had gravity working for us, it could just as easily be destructive if a sled would break loose and go clattering down on the dogs.

Sometimes, when it looked like relatively clear sledding, we would disconnect the dogs from the sled and ride it down, bucking this way and that, like cowboys in an Arctic rodeo. Other times, we would proceed more cautiously, stopping here and there, using ice outcroppings as brakes.

Either way, up or down, putting pressure ridges behind us was hard work, as hard as I've ever done, under the worst conditions I've ever experienced. Imagine having

Frozen lead running east

to push a piano up a staircase and back down again. Then imagine doing that 20 or 25 times a day, in temperatures of 50 below Fahrenheit.

One pressure ridge in particular was difficult for the dogs. We came upon a lead where the ice was actually rubbery. This is yet another phenomenon of the Arctic. It occurs where thin ice has broken up and is beginning to refreeze; the skin of ice that results is sturdy enough to support you, with the Arctic Ocean beneath it, but not sturdy enough to be rigid. Walking across it is like walking across a water bed; as you walk, you rise and fall on a bouncy surface.

Of course, on this kind of terrain, you walk gingerly. As the sled I was guiding made its way across one such stretch, the ice suddenly gave way, and my lead dog and the three others following her fell into the water.

The remaining five dogs knew to stop. I rushed forward, seized the tug line and began working to pull the dogs out of the black water. As I pulled, I realised I was creating additional force against the ice. Almost immediately, I plunged in up to my waist. The only reason I wasn't totally submerged was that I instinctively maintained my hold on the tug line.

Talk about a scrotum-shriveling experience! I mean, FUH-HUCK ME!!!!!

It was an intense feeling of absolute shock and overwhelming panic. Four months earlier, during our training session at Schurke's Wintergreen Lodge when we were obliged to ski with our gear into the frozen White Iron Lake, I was able to climb out of the hole in the ice and run the 200 yards to the warmth of sauna.

Here, I had no ski poles to use as ice picks to help me pull myself back out and onto the ice. I knew, too, that I couldn't wait for any help from the crew, if for no other reason than the fact that any additional weight on the ice would mean more pressure, which could spill everyone into the drink.

My only thought was to get out and get out any way I could. Still grasping the tug line, I pulled it and finagled with my other arm to slide up onto the ice. I got up in fairly short order, which was encouraging.

But just as quickly, my mind began weighing the potential consequences of the situation. I was stiff and sore from the rigours of the journey so far, so it took me about half a minute to pull myself fully from the water. My major concern, honestly, was that I would get frostbite or do damage to my bits. I would later learn that uncircumcised Arctic travellers have an advantage in this regard. Specifically, the muscle fibres in the foreskin contract in extreme cold, keeping the bit inside warmer, providing additional protection from frostbite.

My inclination was to change into dry clothing then and there. Schurke had a different idea. He told me to ski hard for half an hour to wick off the water I'd taken on. I didn't argue. I trusted his experience – adding one additional measure of my own. To protect my most precious parts, I stuffed a couple of fleece hats into my pants, thinking they would absorb additional moisture while providing a modicum of warmth. Then I began skiing like crazy, as hard as I had ever skied in my life.

As I skied, the water on the inner layers of my clothing did indeed wick away to the outer layers, where it immediately turned into a thin crust of ice. As I continued to ski, that crust of ice broke apart and fell away.

I dried out quickly enough from the waist down. The only issue was with my boots. An hour after I'd fallen into the drink, the team paused long enough for me to change my socks and put plastic bags between my outer socks and my boot.

As the team continued on its way, I felt invigorated by the experience. One of my greatest fears going into the expedition was that I would fall into the water. My mind was filled with questions about how I would respond, what I would do, how I would get through it if it were to happen.

Randy (The Ice Man) Swanson

And here it had happened. There I was on the other side, with the answers to those questions. With those answers came a feeling of considerable satisfaction. It was one of those experiences where you discover that the anticipation of an object of fear is often worse than the actuality.

Later that night, after we made camp, I polished the experience over and over again in my mind. I thought of the hardships Crozier endured following the summer of 1845, when the British Admiralty launched yet another attempt to find the Northwest Passage using the veteran ice ships, Erebus and Terror. Crozier captained the Terror and was second in command of the expedition, behind the relatively inexperienced John Franklin.

No plans were made for rescue or relief in case the expedition failed to complete its mission within the three years for which it had been supplied. Those supplies, by the way, included 61,987 kilograms of flour, 16,749 litres of liquor, 909 litres of "wine for the sick," 4,287 kilograms of chocolate, 3,214 kilograms of tobacco and 4,200 kilograms of lemon juice to stave off scurvy.

Under Franklin's command, the 129 men who entered the Arctic waterways on the two ships would never be seen again. Diaries found a decade later indicate that Franklin died in 1847 – he was one of the first officers to die – and that command of the expedition had passed to Crozier.

By then, both ships had been crushed to splinters in the ice. The harrowing, hopeless task of leading some 100 survivors across the ice fell to Crozier. On their march, many crewmen dropped dead on the trail. Others resorted to cannibalism in their desperate struggle to survive.

Inuit legend has it that a handful of Crozier's men somehow managed to stay alive for years but never found their way back to civilization. Crozier is thought to have been one of the last to perish.

Over the next few years, nearly 50 ships sailed north in attempts to rescue the lost men. One such party discovered a short account of the expedition containing a message from Crozier describing the attempt to march across the ice to safety.

As I thought of Crozier, I was grateful for the advantages of modern fabrics and cold-weather technology. In the early days of Arctic exploration, back in Crozier's days, a baptism such as I had experienced could easily have proven fatal or at least spelled the beginning of the end.

And of course, it could have been the end of my expedition, not to mention the end of my dear old willard. Instead, I had survived my Arctic baptism.

Cold and tired

"Pushed thru the door. ...

as you couldn't tell the ...

snow and the sky. "Visib-

No depth of field at," at

you was ever sketchy."

"Pushed thru the day. Definitely miserable,
as you couldn't tell the difference between
the snow and the sky. Visibility was
extremely poor. No depth of field at all.
Four feet in front of you was even sketchy."

from Craig Kurz' journal

Chapter 9

A DAY IN THE ARCTIC

My first thought each morning was to hope that the drifting ice had not subtracted much from the previous day's progress. In the Arctic spring, the ice is constantly breaking up, shifting south. Vast shelves of ice the size of small countries have nowhere to go but south. More ice forms as old ice shifts to the south, like scales on a fish or teeth in a shark's maw, so as you move forward, you are traversing a slippery slope indeed.

The net effect is that heading north toward the pole during that time of year, which is really the only time to attempt it, is very much like trying to climb upstairs on a down escalator.

Each day began with a struggle to get dressed inside our sleeping bags. Our bags were rated to minus-50 degrees, and each bag was slipped into a Gore-Tex bivy sack to minimize the condensation of moisture from our breath on the bags themselves.

You've probably had the experience of trying to put on damp clothing. It was something I hated when I was younger. But there I was, fighting to pull on items of clothing while desperately trying to thaw them out as quickly as possible. It was an awkward, cumbersome process.

It meant poking our arms through sleeves that were frozen shut and legs through trousers as stiff as boards.

Makwa catching some zzzz

We kept our socks on for the entire trek and pulled our boots inside our sleeping bags each night, so they would be only slightly frozen. Schurke had warned us that, if we left our boots outside our sleeping bags, they would be frozen solid and virtually impossible to thaw.

If there's an advantage to putting on clothing that's ice cold, it's that you wake up quickly. You're also motivated to get moving.

In the photographs of Admiral Peary and his crew shortly after the turn of the 20th century, it is evident that they wore bulky parkas made from animal skins, with fur-trimmed hoods. With the benefit of advanced science, modern polar explorers dress in multiple thin layers.

In the morning, when we were getting started, we would wear the greatest number of layers. As the day continues, the body acts as a furnace, heating up as you confront each new challenge. We found ourselves removing layers or unsnapping vents in our clothing as we went.

I began each day of the expedition with four layers on my upper body – a base of thermal underwear, followed by a light fleece, then a thin wind shell, topped off with a thick jacket padded with plenty of goose feather insulation.

On the lower half of my body, I wore a pair of thermal long johns and rip-stop nylon snow pants.

On my feet, I wore a light pair of socks, then a heavy pair, then boot liners. My calf-high insulated Sorrell boots were made of canvas with thick rubber soles. They made my feet look twice their actual size. But they kept them warm and dry.

Good frozen lead
running north

Ice rubble makes
progress slow and
dangerous

I wore two layers of thin gloves, topped with a thick wind-check glove. To protect my eyes from the brilliant reflection of the sun off the snow and potential snow blindness, I wore sunglasses with an ultra-high polarization factor and side vision blinders for extra protection.

To protect our faces from windburn and frostbite, each team member carried a role of adhesive moleskin, which we would stick to our cheeks, brows and noses.

One adjustment I made after my Arctic baptism was to stuff one of my fleece caps into my underwear – the idea being to guard against frostbite on the one extremity I would hate to lose above all others.

One additional point about clothing:

Most of us kept most of our layers on for the duration of the trip. Under normal conditions, we undoubtedly would have developed serious body odour. But in the frozen North, odour-causing bacteria has no chance of surviving. So it never mattered if any of us were downwind from the others.

Once we were dressed, we stepped outside the tent. The first order of business was to find an ice rock, preferably one large enough to afford some privacy while we performed our morning constitutionals. If we couldn't find such a spot, we found after a couple days that we were able to put our inhibitions aside.

I'm often asked about how one manages certain bodily functions in the Arctic. During an interview for Ulster television, I was asked point blank, "How did you go to the bathroom?"

My answer: Very quickly. We squatted, wiped with snowballs and got moving as quickly as possible. I will add here that the experience of relieving oneself under those painfully frozen conditions invariably evoked wistful memories of casually perusing the headlines of the day while seated regally on a porcelain throne in cosy surroundings, all at a leisurely pace.

Having made our morning deposits in the snow bank, we would undertake our assigned tasks. While one pair of teammates filled a pair of aluminum cooking kettles with snow and put them on propane fuel burners to make water for breakfast, others would start taking down the tents and prepare to break camp.

It was up to Swanson and me to harness the dogs and get them ready for the trail.

This was no small undertaking. The dogs would be fully rested and eager to get going. Instead of politely standing for the harness, they jumped and thrashed about wildly, so that we burned up quite a lot of energy getting them ready. I usually found myself removing my first layer of the day at this point.

Then an amazing transformation would occur. One moment, the dogs would be barking and howling, straining at the traces while team members scrambled about bumping into one another. Utter chaos.

Then Schurke would give the signal to move out and, in an instant, the scene changed completely. The dogs would go silent, and the energy of the time team would focus on moving forward, toward our goal.

As long as you're moving in the Arctic, for the most part, you can stay warm. Each of us slogged along in silent solitude, whether on skis or walking alongside the sleds. Occasionally, a team member would ski alongside for a mile or so, and you'd have a chat.

But for the most part, we concentrated on moving forward at a good pace, each of us on his or her own.

While the human members of our team were afforded the luxury of stopping when we had to relieve ourselves, it was a different story for the dogs. When one of them had to go, he would be dragged along by the other dogs, strung from his harness while he did his business. He'd finish, find his feet and continue on the way.

Schurke would decide when we had reached the end of the day. He based his decision on how troublesome the trail had been, how many miles we'd put behind us and how spent we were.

There were many times, of course, when he would say, "Just another mile." Three miles later, it would be "just another mile" again. He liked to put us up against a pressure ridge to afford us shelter from the wind. After 10 to 12 hours on the trail, when he finally would find a suitable campsite, it was always a relief. I don't remember a single time where any of us said, "Wah! Let's not stop just yet. Can't we put in a couple more hours?"

We convened in the cook tent for dinner. I had brought a Walkman tape player and a pair of miniature speakers, along with an assortment of recordings by U2, Thin Lizzy, Van Morrison and other Irish rockers. These provided the musical accompaniment for our dinner.

The conversation would meander from the events of the day to how far we had come and how far we still had to go. Then, fairly quickly after we had finished our meal, we would crawl off in our tents. For me at least, sleep would come in next to no time at all.

And now there came both
it grew wondrous cold:
ice, mast-high, came flo[...]
As green as emerald.

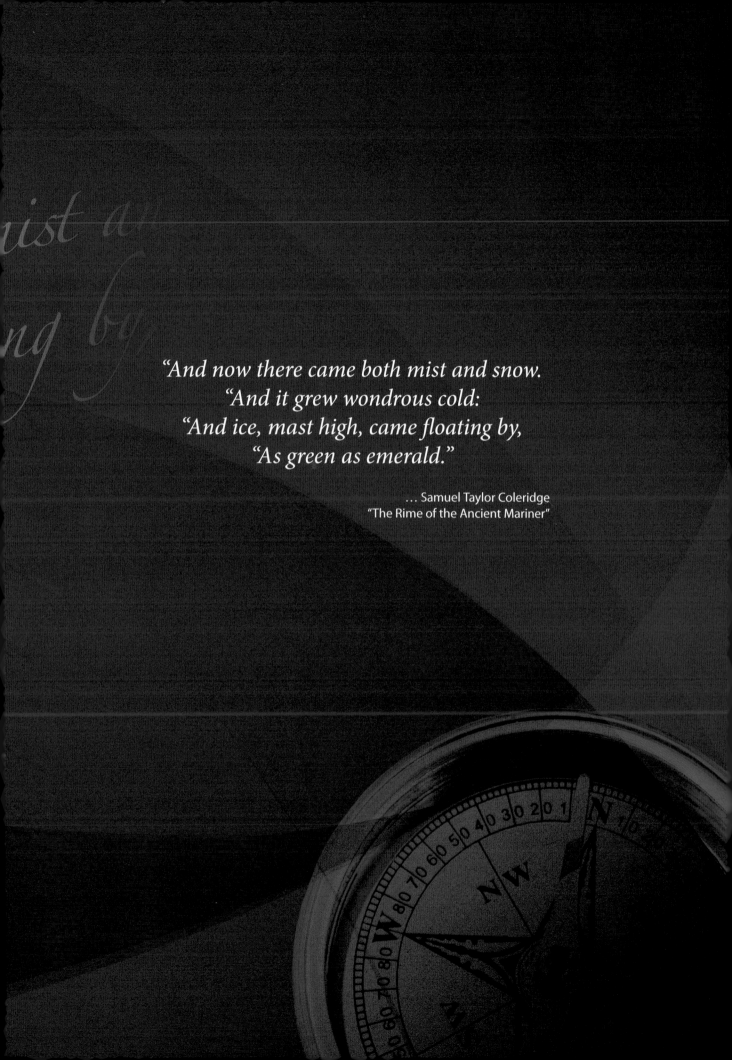

"And now there came both mist and snow.
"And it grew wondrous cold:
"And ice, mast high, came floating by,
"As green as emerald."

… Samuel Taylor Coleridge
"The Rime of the Ancient Mariner"

Chapter 10

ARCTIC IDYLLS

As we continued on through the snow and the ice, I passed by scenes of amazing beauty and experienced sights for which none of my readings had prepared me.

When the winds were calm, the snow glittered and sparkled with a brightness more dazzling than anything I'd ever seen. Here and there, the ice glowed with an unearthly green or blue.

At one point, while we were stopped for one of our hourly breaks, I looked up and saw the sun in three places, aligned in a horizontal row. I was seeing a phenomenon variously known as a sundog or parhelia. They occur when sunlight is refracted by ice in the atmosphere, creating the illusion of a pair of brightly coloured spots, one on either side of the sun.

Sundogs are visible when the sun is near the horizon and on the same horizontal plane as the observer and the ice crystals. As sunlight passes through the ice crystals, it bends by 22 degrees before reaching the eye. The bending is what creates the spots.

The brightest parhelia occur on cold sunny mornings or evenings, when the sun is closest to the horizon and the air is filled with ice crystals.

Swanson and me

At other times, when we were crossing over where an open lead of water had refrozen, I found myself walking through Arctic meadows of delicate ice formations that would be four or five inches tall, in the shape of small ferns.

I also discovered that, even on firm ice, it was possible to get a feeling that was almost like being seasick. I experienced a brief bout of it travelling across a stretch of ice waves, as we called them. Ice waves are formed when long expanses of ice break apart and refreeze. When the wind

Taking five

picks up across the break in the ice, the water ripples up into waves. A sudden drop in temperature can cause these waves to turn to ice, retaining their rolling shape. Surfing these frozen waves on cross-country skis or alongside a dog sled is very much like driving across a surface dimpled with lots of small speed bumps.

Oh, and there's one more curiosity that apparently at least has little to do with ice, if anything. I mention elsewhere here that, to keep up our energy stores, we were obliged to consume 6,000 calories each day and still managed to lose 26 pounds by the time our trek was concluded. All of us lost weight.

But even at that, most of us experienced a phenomenon we called "Arctic bloat." The parts of our bodies that were more exposed to the cold, our faces and hands, swelled up very noticeably. About midway through the expedition, we developed round moon faces and fat fingers.

It's fairly common among mountain climbers who achieve high altitudes – the low pressure at high altitudes can cause a condition called high altitude pulmonary oedema, which is often accompanied by a feeling of nausea, known as high-altitude sickness.

But we were travelling at sea level – or a few feet above sea level, depending on the thickness of the ice. I've spoken with several physicians, including one skilled in wilderness medicine, but I have yet to hear an adequate explanation for our Arctic bloat. For now, at least, it's another mystery of the Great White North.

The cold journey is taking its toll

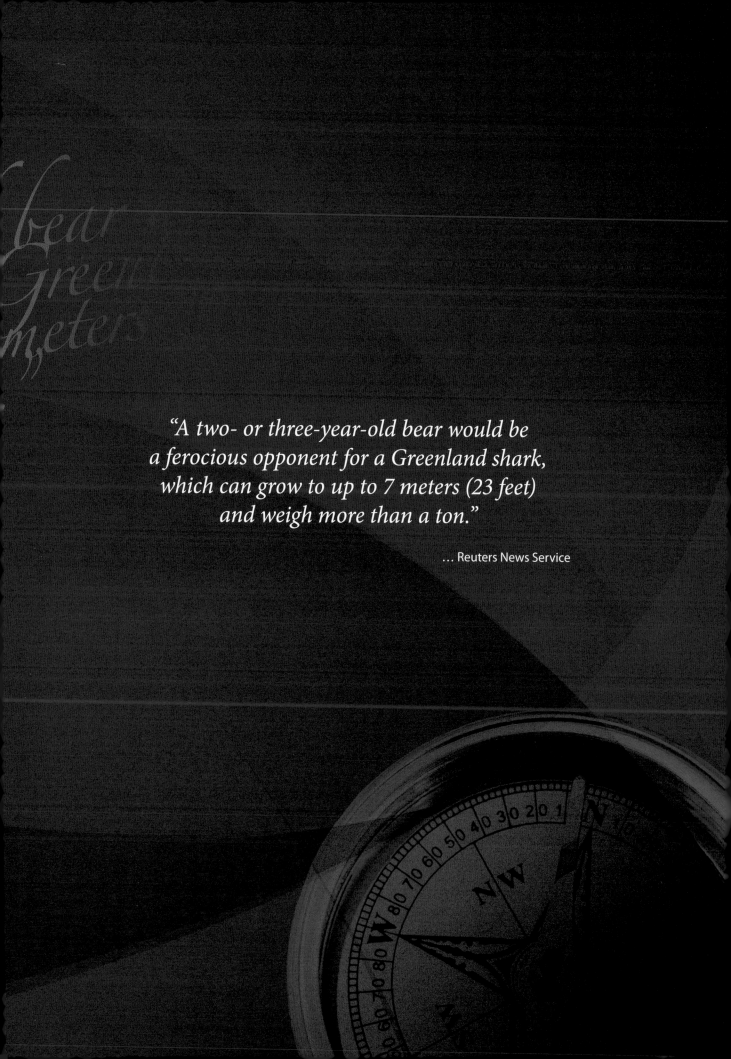

"A two- or three-year-old bear would be
a ferocious opponent for a Greenland shark,
which can grow to up to 7 meters (23 feet)
and weigh more than a ton."

... Reuters News Service

Chapter 11

WE AREN'T ALONE

There is a personality to the Arctic, a spirit that is by turns compelling and malevolent, majestic and brutal. You can hear it in the wind and see it in the incredible beauty of a constantly changing landscape. You can feel it in the inescapable cold that seems to grip you and the swirling vertigo of the whiteouts that envelop you.

Different people have different names for it. I call it polargeist. Whatever you call it, it's a personality with different facets.

Sometimes, it's a mischievous gremlin. I remember it manifesting itself with the Aspiration Expedition many times, including one occasion when it seemed to take the form of a gust of wind that ripped a tent from its binding and sent it rolling and tumbling down the ice like the giant white bouncing ball in the opening scenes to the classic British television series, "The Prisoner." Schurke was the only one of us who could ski fast enough to catch up with it, but it took him a good mile of all-out effort to do so.

Bridge building

On another occasions, the dogs somehow were released from their stakeout line. We heard them running about in the middle of the night, too late to prevent them from finding their food cache and eating themselves into a virtual coma, gobbling up several days of grub from an already limited stash.

Other times, such as during the blizzard that made forward progress physical agony, this spirit can be a merciless tormentor; a bully that delights in inflicting fear and pain.

Still other times, it can seem almost to be a guardian angel, a very real presence that puts you at ease, even when the feeling flies in the face of all logic.

Kurts ice bridge crossing

Legendary explorers Tom Crean, Ernest Shackleton and Frank Worsley experienced something very much like polargeist in their epic 1915 journey in an open boat across uncharted territory from Elephant Island to South Georgia. While comparing their diaries of that journey, Shackleton and Worsley both realised they had had a strange feeling there had been a fourth in their party. Crean afterwards confessed to the same feeling.

I know what they meant. Many times, our team members, myself included, felt a presence we couldn't see.

On our fifth day on the ice, we discovered tangible evidence we weren't alone. But this presence was not imagined. It was a physical entity that walked, breathed and hunted – a creature with real blood in its veins.

There in the snow were the tracks of two polar bears – one large set accompanied by a smaller set. Schurke estimated the tracks were two days old. He also said they were the tracks of a male and a female, the larger set probably belonging to a male weighing about 900 pounds. The tracks were about 12 inches wide.

Looking at prints in the snow, I had mixed feelings. On one hand, I would very much have liked to see a polar bear in its natural environment. At the same time, such an occurrence could have presented a considerable danger to the team members, dogs and bear alike.

Normally, it's unusual for a male and female to travel together, unless it's a mother and her cub. And in that case, you'd be more likely to see three or four sets of tracks, because polar bears generally have two or three cubs at a time.

But this time of year, spring in the Arctic extending through mid-May, is the polar bear's mating season. As with most species, male bears are more aggressive during that part of their life cycle than at any other time. For the most part, polar bears are motivated by curiosity. Even when they get into a scrap over a seal carcass, one of

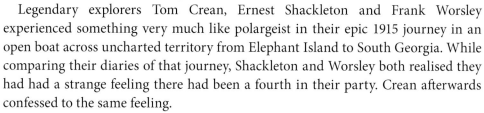

(N)ice moustache!

them will usually walk away before it escalates into anything too serious. That's not the case during mating season.

It wasn't likely we would actually encounter any bears – they're known to be shy of sled dogs. Still, Schurke decided it would be a good idea to test our bear protection system. He fired a round from the .308-caliber hunting rifle that was packed in one of the sleds.

Then I fired a round from our 20-gauge pump-action shotgun. The butt of the shotgun had been broken off earlier when a sled came crashing down a pressure ridge, so I had to fire it from my hip. Other than that, it was in proper working order.

We took a few photographs, then continued north. As we marched in single file, each of us seemed to follow the one in front more closely. I brought up the rear. After Schurke casually mentioned that polar bears tend to hunt from the rear, I found myself looking over my shoulder more than once.

The sight of those tracks left me with two impressions, each the opposite of the other. They reminded me we weren't alone, yet they reinforced my feeling of just how isolated we were.

It made us all the more grateful for the Iridium pagers Hall had given each of us at the outset of our journey. These pagers were connected with a global satellite system that enabled them to receive email messages from any point on the planet. Through these devices, we could hear from friends and family members back home, although we could not communicate with them.

Hall also had established a website, www.aspirations.com, so that anyone who wished could follow the expedition's progress from one day to the next. Through a public relations firm he hired, Hall also set up links with other media outlets and their websites, including CNN and MSNBC. By the time it was all over, the Aspirations Expedition website and associated links reported a total of 29,065,000 hits.

I'd been concerned when I fell through the water into the ice that I'd damaged my pager. The feeling of hearing it beep and buzz at odd moments as I struggled through one day to the next never failed to lift my spirits above my circumstances. Each message was like a letter from home.

I heard from well-wishers from my hometown of Lisburn, people I'd never met but who were kind enough to take the time to spur me on. Other messages from dear friends and family members meant more to me than I can describe.

I would read each one at least three times. Each gave me warmth and renewed my sense of commitment. Each was another nudge on my way to the pole.

If there really is a robe a
there's some dead explorer
to it.

If there really is a pole at the North Pole, I bet there's some dead explorer guy with his tongue stuck to it.

… Bob Van Voris, Lawyer & Journalist

Chapter 12

THE URINATION OF THE IRIDIUM PHONE

Arctic Cowboy

I was the first one into the cook tent on the morning of April 21, aside from its usual inhabitants, Kurz and Hall. The temperature was a nostril-chilling 38 below. Normally, Kurz would be busily preparing the team's breakfast, and Hall would be yakking on his Iridum satellite telephone to some radio station in the U.S., putting out the word about his experiences on the ice, promoting his Great Aspirations charity.

But on this morning, it was obvious something had gone wrong, horribly wrong. Kurz was not his usual chirpy self, although he had a bit of a smirk. Hall was downright despondent.

I asked what was wrong. Hall replied that moisture had somehow gotten into his Iridium phone, causing it to malfunction. So I asked him how such a thing could have happened. He hemmed and hawed a bit, then said that water had somehow leaked out of his water bottle. As he said it, he looked at the ground, like a child who'd been caught doing something he shouldn't.

I pushed the issue.

"Well, how did that happen?" I asked.

That's when Kurz piped in. "He peed on it," he said.

Hall came clean. What had happened was that, while he was in his sleeping bag the night before, he'd mistaken the phone for his pee bottle and given it a good soaking. The source of moisture, as it turned out, was his bladder.

Hall made it clear he wanted this to be our little secret. I understood his wanting to keep a lid on it. Who could blame him? It would be quite an embarrassment if something like that were to get out to the rest of the team. I told him I'd be right back. Then I stepped out of the tent, cupped my hands to my mouth and hollered out the following announcement:

"Guess what, everybody! The phone's buggered – Doug peed on it!"

I should explain that the Iridium phone had become a bit of an issue with some of the team members. At several points on our trek, we had to stop while Hall used the phone to report the day's

Dogs staked out

events to Wecker back at our base camp.

Wecker would then write an account based on Hall's description on his laptop computer and ship it off to the Scripps Howard News Service, which in turn distributed these dispatches globally.

For the rest of the team, these interludes meant standing around in the freezing cold. One time in particular, Schurke set up a tent so Hall could make his call, while the rest of us shivered in the wind.

Schurke still had his high frequency radio, so we could use it to communicate with the outside world – but just barely, because the radio's signal was highly dependent on ionospheric conditions. The telephone, when it was dry and functioning, transmitted and received far more clearly.

On his first trip to the North Pole in 1986, Schurke encountered a similar problem with his sextant. He was getting mixed readings from one day to the next. His solution was to take the sextant into his tent and take it apart. There between two lenses, he found an ice crystal. He wiped the ice away, cleaned the lenses, and the sextant once again functioned perfectly.

He decided it was worth a shot to take the same approach with Hall's Iridium phone. He took the phone apart and tried wiping its innards dry with toilet paper. Then he reassembled it and tried to dial out. It didn't work. This was, after all, a highly sophisticated piece of technology, not a simple sextant.

But Schurke wasn't ready to give up. He opened the phone's housing, so that it was in two pieces. He put a pan inside a larger pan, then put those inside a still larger pan. In the middle pan, he put the two pieces of the phone on a roll of toilet paper in an effort to insulate them from the direct heat. Then he put the whole thing on the cook stove and lit it. His idea, essentially, was to bake the phone until it was dry.

Incredibly, once the phone was reassembled, it worked again – after a fashion at least. Hall was able to get through to his assistant, Kari McCampbell in Cincinnati. But it was a one-way conversation. She could hear him, but he couldn't hear her. We knew this because she emailed a message to that effect to Hall's pager.

The timing was somewhat propitious, though. As it happened we were planning to arrange to have a Twin Otter drop off a supply of dog food, given that our supply had been diminished a few nights earlier in the episode I described, when the dogs somehow got free from their stake-out line and tore into their stash of grub while we were sleeping.

A flight would soon be coming our way to pick up English explorer Pen Hadow, who had guided a handful of Malaysians to a point about 50 miles from the pole. Schurke recalled that Hadow also had an Iridium phone, so he got on his radio and set about contacting him. At the same time, he was working out arrangements through our base camp manager, Wecker, with Ken Borek Air Ltd. in Resolute.

Such an exchange is far easier said than done. We found a stretch of smooth flat ice, ideal for a plane to land on, and pitched camp beside it.

"It's as flat a strip as I've seen so far," Schurke told Commander Dave over his radio that night.

"Two thousand-plus feet long, single-year ice, about three feet thick, covered with an inch of snow. There are a couple of snow bumps here and there, but nothing more than six inches high."

We hoped for a plane to land the next day. The night sky was a clear, light blue colour. We turned in that night hoping the weather would cooperate.

It didn't. We awoke on our eighth day on the ice to a heavy cloud cover, with a ceiling of about 1,000 feet, eliminating any possibility of a landing. By the time the plane's pilot broke through the clouds and got a look at our landing strip, he wouldn't have had any time to get his bearings in order to land the plane safely.

We broke camp and slogged on for another day. That evening, while the team was making camp again, Schurke found a potential landing strip about a mile and a half away.

Around 3 a.m. that morning, he woke the rest of us. He'd been on the radio, listening as one of Borek's planes had picked up Hadow and his companions at the pole. In the process, Schurke decided to find a longer strip. He'd done some scouting and found what looked like a good spot half a mile away from camp.

He called us on the walkie-talkie. Some of the team members hustled in that direction to meet the plane. When they got there, they learned the pilot had decided to land at a different spot. So they all hurried over there and, finally, they were able to complete the rendezvous.

Hadow handed his phone over to Hall, who promptly phoned in his report for the day to Wecker back in Resolute. The deal Hall struck with Hadow was to rent the phone for $10,000. It was a classic case of supply and demand in action. Hall assured Hadow that Commander Dave would pay him upon his return to Resolute, using a $40,000 stash in a Zip-Loc bag that Hall had entrusted him with for just such a contingency.

Once more, our line of communication was open. Soon, we were back on the trail, continuing our march toward our goal.

What 30 below feels like

Talk of your cold! through the parka's fold
it stabbed like a driven nail.
If our eyes we'd close, then the lashes froze til
sometimes we couldn't see ...

From "The Cremation of Sam McGee"
By Robert Service

Chapter 13

THE WEIGHT OF THE COLD

The Arctic grinds at the human spirit. The endless white, the relentless cold, the howling wind, the inescapable sense of isolation, the obstacles that rise up at every turn – these are factors that conspire to undermine fortitude, erode resolve and gnaw away at purpose. The top of the world is strewn with tales of despair.

One story widely circulated among Resolute locals is of a psychologist who came through the Polar Continental Shelf Project to undertake a study of the effects of long periods of isolation on the human psyche. He endured two months of Arctic isolation himself before he was heard one day on the high frequency radio babbling and begging to be airlifted back to civilization.

Cold has an anaesthetic property that can have horrifying effects. Soldiers during the retreat of Napoleon's army from Moscow in the winter of 1812 used their horses as walking food sources. It was too cold to butcher them outright – one, because the soldiers' hands were too numb and, two, because the meat would have frozen hard as bricks. August Thirion, senior sergeant of the 2nd Cuirassiers, Napoleon's mounted cavalry soldiers, described this scenario:

"We cut a slice from the quarters of horses still on their feet and walking, and these wretched animals gave not the least sign of pain, proving beyond doubt the degree of numbness and insensitivity caused by the extreme cold.

Storm coming

Getting close

"Under any other conditions, these slices of flesh would have brought on a haemorrhage, but this did not occur with 28 degrees of frost. The blood froze instantly, and this congealed blood arrested the flow. We saw some of these poor horses walking for several days with large pieces of flesh cut away from both thighs."

In the same way, many casualties who'd had arms or legs blown off during the Falklands conflict in 1982 survived despite not being able to reach field hospitals for many hours because the intense cold dramatically reduced the blood loss. This in turn brought on a mild hypothermia that reduced their bodies' need for oxygen, which enabled these men to survive despite their reduced blow flood.

Last camp

It was colder than that where we were. On our sixth day on the ice, one member of our team experienced an emotional and physical breakdown. His collapse cast a shadow over the entire expedition.

Contributing to the episode was the realization we were losing ground while we slept. Through the rotation of the earth and the shifting of the ice from north to south, we were losing anywhere from a quarter of a mile to 10 miles overnight.

On a good day, under optimal conditions and with maximum effort, we could manage 16 miles. So you can imagine that the thought of losing any ground at all was a blow to morale.

On one occasion, in fact, we woke up further back than we were when we set out the prior morning. This knowledge, coupled with the relentless cold and all

Final Stretch

the other perils of travelling through the Arctic, made it all that much more difficult to persevere.

Our sixth day began innocently enough, although we could see dark clouds in the distance. The morning light made it appear as if the clouds and snow were merged on the horizon. We had a quiet breakfast, packed our gear and hit the ice shortly before 8 a.m. It was then we noticed that one of our team seemed not to be with us.

Golibersuch was moving much more slowly than the rest of us. He was listless, almost unresponsive. Of all the members of our team, he was the least fit from the outset. I had not understood from our first meeting four months earlier at Schurke's Wintergreen Lodge why he had been accepted onto the team. It struck me then that he could become a liability.

At 56, Golibersuch said he'd done a bit of cross-country skiing to get in shape for our trip, but little else. Once on the ice, it turned out he was not a good skier. Since then, he'd been going downhill day by day. He was the first of our team to develop frostbite. The tips of his fingers and toes were black, oozing and raw.

What had happened was that water molecules in his skin cells had frozen. In the early stages of frostbite, affected areas take on a white, waxy appearance and feel numb and hard to the touch.

Frostbite occurs when the body loses more heat than it generates in the body's natural effort to maintain its normal temperature. Essentially, frostbite happens at the appendages when the body decides to risk or even sacrifice its more expendable parts, like fingers and toes, in order to preserve its core temperature and avoid death from hypothermia. The extremities cool down in an attempt to keep the body temperature where it needs to be.

To keep the toes and digits at normal body temperature, greater blood flow is required, which in turn sends cooled blood back to the body core, cooling the body even more. The extremities have a high surface area/volume ratio, so they lose heat very easily. So fingers and toes are first to go. Noses are a close second.

More severe cases of frostbite result in a bluish black colour, which was the situation with Golibersuch. Left untreated, frostbite can lead to gangrene and require amputation.

I was not the only one in our group to wonder if Golibersuch should be airlifted out, but we weren't in charge – Schurke was. And in fairness, the journey was taking its toll on all of us. Most members of the team were dealing with frostbitten fingers, toes and noses as we headed north with our faces in the cutting wind. Some of us were walking on twisted ankles.

Then the storm hit. It came at 1 p.m. on our seventh day on the ice. Winds gusting up to 50 miles per hour caused the temperature to plummet and quickly created whiteout conditions.

Wind makes cold colder. American explorer Paul Siple is credited with coining the term, "wind-chill factor," as a metric for the ability of wind to increase the rate of heat loss, basically because wind replaces warm surface air with cold.

Siple conducted a series of simple experiments in Antarctica in 1941 in which he compared the time it took for baked-bean tins filled with water to freeze at different temperatures and with different wind velocities. Their observations led to a formula that estimates the cooling power of wind by way of a "wind-chill equivalent temperature."

In still air of minus 29 degrees Celsius (or minus 20 degrees Fahrenheit), the danger for a person who is properly dressed is relatively small. But if the wind kicks up to only 10 miles an hour, the temperature equivalent drops to minus 44 C (or minus 42 F), at which point skin will freeze within a couple minutes. Jump that to a 25-mile-an-hour wind, and flesh freezes within 30 seconds.

I felt as if my face was being sandblasted and flash-frozen at the same time. The wind chipped away at the snow and ice, flinging it against my face so hard it stung like tiny BBs. It felt as if the skin was being torn away from my skull. All day long, we trudged along in those conditions, one foot forward, then the other, on and on. It was sheer misery, but our only choice was to keep moving forward.

The wind was blowing so hard and the snow flying so thick and heavy that it was impossible to see where the sky ended and the horizon began. If the bright red anorak of the team member marching in front of me drifted more than 10 feet away, I lost sight of it

It was an absolute horror. With each step, I had no idea what I was stepping on. At one point, Schurke got so far ahead of the lead sled that the dogs could no longer see him. We knew that because they had been following him all along. Now they were stopping, looking this way and that, not sure which way to go. It was a sickening feeling, I can tell you, when they stopped and turned, as if they were looking to us for direction. It was as discouraging a moment as any of us had had on our punishing journey up to that point.

By the time we set up camp, we had somehow covered another 10 miles. We huddled in our tents with the wind howling throughout the night, as if daring us to continue. We sat there, each of us staring blankly into our own private spaces, too exhausted to do much more than breathe.

Schurke set about to making arrangements over the radio to have a Ken Borek Air Ltd. flight drop in on us with more dry soup mix and dog food to replenish what the dogs had gobbled up when they broke loose from their line a few days earlier, leaving them perilously short of grub.

The same flight would be carrying English Arctic guide Pen Hadow, the English Arctic guide I mentioned earlier, who had agreed to rent his Iridium phone to Hall, replacing the global phone he had shorted out through the confusion between it and the pee bottle in his sleeping bag. When Hadow arrived back in Resolute a few days later, he immediately looked up Wecker, who dutifully forked over the dough from the Zip-Loc bag in which it had been presented to him.

Around 3 a.m. the next morning, the pilot located a stretch of ice suitable for a landing. As the plane skied to a stop, Schurke felt a tug at his elbow. It was Golibersuch. With the wind still whipping around him, he waved his Platinum American Express card in Schurke's face and tearfully pleaded to be allowed to climb aboard the Twin Otter.

Schurke wouldn't allow it. I think I would be speaking for the rest of the team to say we would have been glad to see Golibersuch go, for his sake as much as our own.

During a telephone conversation later that night with Wecker back in Resolute, Schurke gave this account:

"With the blustery conditions and the frustrations of encountering one obstacle after another, it's been difficult sledding for us all day every day. For some of us, the emotional highs and lows have been quite extreme.

"In the case of Dave (Golibersuch), he injured his ankle early on and has since taken some pretty severe frostbite. His physical condition, along with the rigours of 12- and sometimes 14-hour travel days, took a mental toll as well.

"In the middle of a windstorm, Dave hit the wall. A dog sled pulled up alongside me, and there was Dave, spread-eagled across it in a hypothermic delirium. We couldn't stop at that point. At the risk of sounding melodramatic, to stop up here in a windstorm is to die.

"You simply have to keep moving."

The initial symptoms of hypothermia include shivering, mild confusion and lethargy. If body temperature keeps falling – which it will do automatically once you stop moving, because your body stops creating its own heat – the symptoms grow increasingly severe, until victims are unable to perform even the simplest motor functions.

That's where Golibersuch was. His speech was slurred, and he was behaving irrationally. In extreme cases, when the body's temperature drops to 90 degrees, victims have been known to tear off their clothing. The heart rate and breathing slow to a crawl. Full heart failure is just a step away.

The team had no option but to get Golibersuch moving again, both for his sake and ours, so his body could once again begin generating warmth. Schurke and other team members got him up on his feet and hooked one of his arms through the handlebar of a dog sled. The idea was to get his legs moving. But instead of walking, Golibersuch put his feet on the sled runners and just managed to hold on, which meant he wasn't creating any body heat.

"I remember feeling just miserable," Golibersuch would say later.

"And I remember the other folks suggesting I ride one of the sleds for a while. At one point, I remember Randy Swanson walking arm in arm with me, talking about his kids, telling me about his hobbies."

Swanson may well have saved Golibersuch's life – along with various other team members who took turns walking with him, coaching him along. A couple hours later at camp that evening, Golibersuch was helped into a tent, where his frostbite was treated. He said he remembered sitting down, trying to get up, being unable to move.

"That's when I lost it completely. I was mumbling, shivering, shaking and crying like a baby, totally out of control. I was aware of what I was doing, but I couldn't stop. It was like nothing I'd ever experienced – a deep black hole of depression, desperation and misery."

The other team members helped him change into warmer clothes, then put him in a sleeping bag with three hot water bottles, one under each armpit and one at his crotch, and fed him a few bowls of soup.

"What helped me more than anything was the human touch of having the folks patting my back, talking to me and telling me that there are a lot of people pulling for me," Golibersuch would recall.

He slept soundly that night. The next day, the expedition moved 13.9 miles closer to its goal. It was the team's best travel day to date.

"Less than 24 hours later, Dave was back in full form," Schurke told Wecker during the nightly call to our base camp back in Resolute.

"He actually led the way part of the time and helped to blaze the trail. Taking a pretty serious down, and coming back the way he did – it wasn't just a victory for Dave. It was a victory for us all."

That's not the way I remember it. It wasn't exactly like Golibersuch bounced back; it was more that he managed to get one foot in front of the other for the rest of the trip. Hearing a 56-year-old man crying like a child was demoralizing, to say the least.

The episode raised questions about Schurke's leadership. Why didn't he let Golibersuch leave on the plane? On the day of the whiteout, why did he get so far ahead of us? If one of us had gotten lost in the blizzard, what could he have done?

As it was, none of us did get lost. And Golibersuch, although he was in pain, did finish the trip – with the help of other team members, Swanson in particular.

Golibersuch's frostbite had advanced to the point that he was unable to perform the most basic of human functions. When he had to relieve himself, Swanson realised it and took him aside. He reached into Golibersuch's trousers and pulled out his penis so he could urinate without getting it all over himself. For the rest of the trip, Swanson helped Golibersuch in that regard and others.

In his own way, Schurke helped Golibersuch make it through as well – if only because he didn't allow Golibersuch an option. Maybe he was right not to allow Golibersuch to leave on that plane. As it turned out, I believe Golibersuch may have come away with the most valuable lesson of any of us on that trip. He learned a measure of humility I don't believe he had before his breakdown.

I also believe Schurke took a risk in making the decision he did. But leaders have to make decisions, which means they have to take risks. It's what being a leader means. In the final analysis, if his leadership had to be summed up in a headline, it might read like this:

He got us there, and he got us back – all of us.

Later on, when we were back at Resolute, waiting to return to Edmonton and then back to our homes, we joked about which of us would get Golibersuch's big toe, if indeed it would have to be amputated. I mentioned that I would like to have it for a key fob. Commander Dave said he thought it would be attractive on a necklace.

We were laughing, enjoying glass after glass of red wine, having a great time. Golibersuch was laughing, too. And I remember thinking that despite all of it – the endless white, the relentless cold, the howling wind, the sense of isolation – we could laugh again.

We'd accomplished our goal. And we'd proven something, if only to ourselves.

"Life's a voyage that's homeward bound."

… Herman Melville

Chapter 14

THE HOME STRETCH

We were 10 miles away from our destination. The temperature stood at a marrow-chilling 25 below. If all went well, we would arrive at the North Pole with one more day of travel to go. But even at that, getting there was by no means a sure thing.

The day before, Bill Martin had sustained a significant injury. He was descending a pressure ridge when his foot became wedged between blocks of ice. His momentum kept his body moving forward, but his leg was held tight. The initial diagnosis was that he might have ruptured a disc or at least torn ligaments in his back.

In any case, he was clearly in agony. When he tried skiing the following morning, he was able to go only about half a mile before the pain prevented him from going any farther. We packed him into a sleeping bag, lifted him onto one of the sleds and continued on our way.

Now, on the morning of what we hoped would be our final day before reaching the pole, the team was most definitely feeling the effects of fatigue, stress and extreme cold.

Most of us were dealing with frostbitten fingers, toes and noses as we continued to head north with our faces in the cutting wind. At least two of us – Hall and myself – had broken through the ice and fallen into the water. Kurz had broken through twice, once thigh-deep and the other, up to his other knee.

It was clear to all of us that the Arctic Ocean wouldn't yield the Pole easily. It seemed we had to improvise at every turn.

An hour after breaking camp, we saw bands of black lines in the sky, parallel to the horizon – a sign of leads, or places where plates of ice have pulled apart, leaving open water. The black water of leads was reflected against the thin stratus clouds as black horizontal stripes.

The first lead was 20 feet across, bordered on either side by walls of ice rising straight up six feet. We skied along the lead for a mile or so until we came upon a place where

Eureka Base on Ellesmere Island

a slab of ice was choking the gap and had frozen in place. Using our skis as chisels, we chipped away at the snow walls to open a passageway. Then we drove our sleds across on the bridge of ice.

A few miles later, we came across a lead 15 feet wide where the ice was moving and shaking under our feet. This was accompanied by a rumbling sound, like the ignition of a tractor-trailer trying to start.

Schurke explained in his call to Wecker that night what was happening:

"The ice plates were grinding against each other, moving with the currents and the wind. It created a shearing action, heaving up splinters of ice eight to 12 feet thick."

Then we hit a huge lead that must have been 150 across. The ice was marshy, and open water stretched out in either direction as we approached it.

It was cold enough that a thin skin of rubbery ice had formed, but it was pulling apart again near the middle of the gap. Schurke led the way, probing with his ski poles as he went. We bobbed up and down with each step on its flexible surface as we followed.

At the gap, where even the rubbery ice was pulling apart, we slid one of the shorter tow sleds forward so that it spanned the open water. We scrambled across the sled, pulling the dogs and the larger sled across from the far side.

In all, we crossed 10 leads that day. It was the most active ice we encountered in our time on the frozen Arctic Ocean.

Those of us with hand-held Global Positioning Systems began counting down the distance when we were about two miles away from the Pole.

Schurke told us he would fire off a flare when he reached the one-mile point, then skied on ahead. The team members found themselves shaking off the toll the trail had taken on them, picking up the pace as we came ever closer.

Suddenly in the distance, we saw a streak of vertical light shoot into the sky. A split second later, we heard the crack of Schurke's flare. Unfortunately, so did the dogs – and it terrified them. They reacted like most dogs do in the presence of fireworks. In this case, they immediately did a 180, heading south for all they were worth.

By this time, the sleds were considerably lighter, having shed most of their weight, and it was a good 200 yards before we could pull the dogs to a halt, Swanson on the sled carrying Martin, myself on the other.

We got the sleds turned around and, at 8:27 p.m. Monday, April 26, 1999, with the oldest member of our team, 69-year-old Peterson skiing in the lead, we reached our destination: 90 degrees north, where we finally were able to stand on the shadow of the bird flying overhead.

How can I tell you what the feeling was like? It was something I'd dreamed about from the time I was a boy, waiting for the first snow to fall. It was a dramatic, emotional, exuberant moment.

We were all thinking about our families and loved ones. I found myself thinking about my older brother, Bill, who had died in a motorcycle accident nearly 20 years earlier. In a way I can't quite explain, standing there on top of the world, I almost felt like I could reach out to him.

At that moment, with every person and every living thing south of me, I had a sense that the world was spinning beneath my feet. It was as if the polargeist I spoke of earlier had taken on a joyful, peaceful demeanour. There seemed to be no cold, no aching muscles, no fatigue. It was a feeling of victory that I am sure will stay with me the rest of my days.

I made a conscious effort to make mental notes so the memory of the moment would be etched into my mind.

With our ski poles, we wrote our names in the snow, along with the names of our family members, friends, anyone who was important to any one of us.

We spent 15 minutes celebrating. There were tears of jubilation as we exchanged congratulations, slapped one another on the back and took turns snapping each other's photos.

Schurke let us have our little celebration, then told us it was time to move on beyond the pole, since the ice was drifting against us at a rate of a tenth of a mile each hour.

We also had to keep moving to find a suitable landing area for the Twin Otter aeroplanes that would carry us and our dogs, sleds and gear to the Canadian weather station at Eureka, then onto Resolute, where we would board other, more conventional aircraft for the trips back to our respective homes.

Schurke scaled a pinnacle of ice to get the lay of the landscape. He hollered back down that he had spotted a stretch of reasonably flat ice a few miles ahead. So we continued on about two more miles toward Siberia and there made camp.

Our hope was that, by the next morning, we would have drifted back to a spot near the Pole. A plane with a half-dozen NASA scientists was to meet us at 90 North. Working with another NASA team stationed at the South Pole, they planned to calculate, for the first time, a precise measurement of the diameter of the earth, using satellite technology.

At about 11 o'clock that night, Schurke phoned the team's base camp with instructions for Wecker to pass along to the people at Ken Borek Air Ltd.:

"Tell them we're sitting on a huge expanse of old ice, with several stretches of 2,000 feet of virtually flat snow and any number of options for a landing strip."

The next morning, when the first plane arrived with the NASA scientists, Elizabeth Arnold of National Public Radio was also on board. She did a 10-minute interview with me for broadcast across America, describing me as the first Irishman to reach either of the poles on foot.

It was at the pole that I met NASA scientist, Mike Cambriati. He was leading a team of genuine rocket scientists who, in conjunction with a second team posted at the South Pole, was working on the experiment I described a few paragraphs earlier.

Cambriati's team also was involved in an experiment called "Cool Space," short for "communications over obscure locations," to establish a satellite link between the poles. He had been with NASA from its earliest days and had become one of its "blue sky" guys – a select group of scientists who dream up experiments and endeavours aimed mostly at seeing what's out there.

Once greetings were exchanged, the first order of business was getting the dogs loaded onto plane and en route to Eureka because our supply of dog food was exhausted.

Swanson and I loaded the dogs and the sled onto the plane, along with our gear and ourselves, and it took off. We stopped at the 86th parallel to refuel at the fuel cache there. Then it was onto Eureka, where we stood once again on solid ground.

As we stepped off the plane, we unloaded the dogs and staked them out. A man from the weather station, located about half a mile away, offered to give us a lift. We happily accepted, thanked him for his kindness and climbed into his pickup truck for the half-mile ride to the base. Later when I was looking over my bill for my stay at Eureka, I saw a charge labelled "Taxi," and a bill for $300. Figuring, 2,640 feet for half a mile, our driver's fare worked out to $1 for every 8.8 feet. So much for Arctic hospitality.

The Eureka base looked like the set from the remake of the horror movie, "The Thing." The buildings were all Quonset huts, equipped with the kind of thick, heavy doors you'd find on heavy-duty industrial deep freezers, complete with freezer door latches instead of knobs.

A man met us at the door and announced the chef had a steak dinner waiting for us, but he insisted we have a shower first. His exact words were, "We've got steak, dinner and apple pie, but the chef's one condition is, you have to get a shower first." When we were on the ice, our collective body odour was contained by the cold. The extreme temperatures prevented bacteria from growing on our body, which is what causes B.O.

Now that we were out of the cold and in the much warmer environment of Eureka, the miniscule fauna inhabiting various crevasses in and around our epidermis were blossoming with a vengeance, and we would soon be quite ripe. That aside, our greeter's words were music to my ears, considering I'd been dining on glops of flavoured pasta and hadn't had a shower for longer than I cared to think about. So naturally, I was feeling more than a little gamey.

It was the best shower I ever had, before or since. I must have stood there letting it wash over me for 40 minutes.

"*The end of the human race will be that it will eventually die of civilization.*"

... Ralph Waldo Emerson

EPILOGUE

I luxuriated for three days at Canada's northernmost weather base in Eureka, hanging fire with Swanson for the plane that would take the dogs back to Resolute Bay, then to Edmonton and home to Ely, Schurke's Minnesota base of operations.

After my shower and an immense steak dinner, followed with apple pie, I had my first sleep in a real bed for the first time in nearly three weeks. I slept soundly for 12 hours.

The next couple days were, for me, filled with the sense of giddiness and sheer joy kids get at Christmas. Clean clothes never felt better, and I had plenty to eat. It might be more accurate to say I descended into an orgy of eating, drinking and television.

Swanson and I spent most of the three days in a pair of lazy-boy-type recliners in the weather station's TV room watching an endless succession of videos.

We were stretched out in those chairs when Wecker arrived at the base. He saw us sitting there, in our almost catatonic state, and observed that it looked like a very heavy but very soft steamroller had rolled over us.

We learned that one of those who had followed our progress on the www. aspirations.com website was Queen Elizabeth. Her telegram to me, relayed through her personal secretary, Andrew Dent, to my sister-in-law, Fiona Humphries in Northern Ireland, read:

"The Queen, who is aware of yesterday's safe arrival of the Expedition from their Web site on the Internet, has asked if you would convey to your brother-in-law and the other members of the team and support group her congratulations and warm good wishes on their memorable achievement."

It was quite an honour to realise we'd drawn the Queen's attention. I would also hear, via my email pager, directly from Tony Blair and Jeffrey Donaldson, my local Member of Parliament, as well former Northern Ireland Secretary of State Mo Mowlam, who invited me for tea at the Royal Residence at Hillsborough.

The transport finally arrived to take us on our next step to the south and closer to home. A few hours later, we were in Resolute, where we deliberated and where Schurke convened a debriefing in which we were all encouraged to talk about our experiences and share our reflections.

We had a bit of a party that evening. Rick Sweitzer, a guide who had arranged for Kurz' parents to make the trip up from Cincinnati, generously presented me a bottle of Irish whisky. Commander Dave and I traded it back and forth, tightly clinging to it each in our turn as if to discourage anyone from asking for a swig. I don't remember much about the evening beyond Swanson's repeated rejections of the advances of two Inuit women with major overbites.

In Edmonton, I bid farewell to the rest of the team and started my way back home via Amsterdam, Manchester and finally Belfast International. There, on May 5, 1999, my family was gathered to welcome me home. There was another party that night, more to celebrate my safe return home than the fact it was my 37th birthday.

And now, years later as I sit here writing these words, I think about what it means to take on a challenge and find the strength to see it through – and how you can draw on that experience for the rest of your life, whether you succeed or not.

The thing is to try. Nothing happens if you don't. That's what I came away with after discovering how it felt to have the world spinning beneath my feet.

90 degrees north

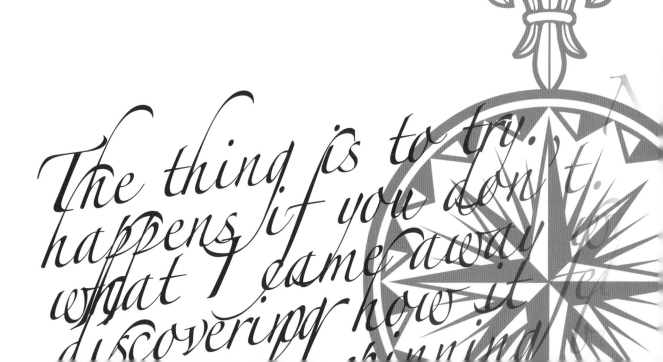